Don't let the title fool you, this is not a 'b stood out for me was the emphasis on relat responsibility each of us must take to make any relationship work. Filled with insights, practical tips, real life stories and timeout questions, Michelle encourages reflection, personal assessment and improvement planning as well as the honesty to consider if it may be time to explore alternate options.

As a Leader or Leader of Leaders, there are important reminders of the privilege and responsibilities held to support and coach others reach their individual or leadership potential, as well as the personal reminder that Leaders never stop needing to develop themselves, reflect and potentially change to get the best out of others.

A book I am sure you will continue to pick up, review based on point-in-time situations, and take ongoing tips from for years to come.

—**Helene Gordon**, Executive General Manager,
People and Communications, Sensis

Bad bosses come at a huge cost for people and productivity, and are a staple of everyday conversation. Yet our conversation about bad bosses often takes the form of blame and externalising — 'if only other people behaved better!' Michelle Gibbings' new book, *Bad Boss*, holds us accountable for how we are all part of the problem — whether we report to a bad boss, manage a bad boss, or are a bad boss — and restores our agency in fixing the problem. This is a book full of insight, compassion and practical suggestions for managing your career, your organisation and yourself.

—**Professor Michael Gilding**, Pro Vice Chancellor, Faculty of
Business and Law, Swinburne University of Technology

Michelle has again delivered a 'must-read' for both leaders and followers of today and tomorrow. There is a huge dose of honesty in this book that is peppered with humour, grounded with stories and thought starters, and filled with wads of common sense. It will challenge you to be better, think differently and own your actions and reactions. It is indeed a book about hope.

—**Angela Green**, Financial Services Executive

We can all relate to stories about a bad boss, but what about when we've been the bad boss? If you have the courage to examine your own blind spots and are driven to change, Michelle's latest book will help you become a better leader.

—**Julia van Graas**, Co-founder, Spiique

Being a follower and having a boss, being a boss, and the boss of bosses are all transformative stages in a potential leadership journey. Michelle's insights will help you to create a roadmap for your transformation into exercising better leadership!

—**Samantha Sharp**, Director of Commissioning and Performance, Western Victoria Primary Health Network

We've all worked for one, we may have had one working for us and if we are brave enough to admit it, we've all been one ourselves from time to time. Yes, you know them, the *Bad Boss*. At its heart this book is about hope and bravery and a must read for anyone who wants to own their journey in developing themselves as a great leader. Michelle expertly sets out easy to implement actions for leaders at any level to apply at any time to turn a bad boss situation into a best boss situation. Michelle's book is packed with advice, anecdotes, and leadership stories that will inspire you to have real conversations, develop and nurture real relationships and be your real you. This is a book that I will refer back to time and again over my leadership journey.

—**Claire Cornfield**, General Manager–Operations, HESTA

Increased day-to-day pressures, longer hours and the challenge of maintaining a positive, diverse workplace are the new norms experienced by employees at any level. Success is achieved through being the best 'you' at work, decisive career development and growing through personal experience to deliver impact. However, this only relates to personal performance. The greater challenge relates to how this translates to the value created by those around you.

The real beauty in *Bad Boss* is that it gives us all the opportunity to turn the mirror on ourselves to assess and challenge ourselves as a leader. Filled with stories, challenging questions and conversation starters, *Bad Boss* allows us to step in the shoes of others in our organisation to consider leadership from different perspectives.

In *Bad Boss*, Michelle provides a comprehensive toolkit to build awareness of personal success drivers, but also fashion shifts and adjustments to create cohesive, high-performing teams that multiply value creation and increase engagement. As in her previous books, Michelle does this in an easy to follow, relatable and intuitive way, applicable to almost any relationship-driven workplace challenge.

—**Richard Benjamin**, Group Director–Strategy, Urbis

It's a familiar saying that 'people don't leave bad jobs, they leave bad bosses'. If you have ever complained or thought about leaving your job because of your boss or have a sneaking suspicion that maybe you are a bad boss or could be a better boss, then this is the book for you.

Michelle's book, *Bad Boss*, is a wonderfully astute and practical guide in helping to deal with or improve your relationship with your boss. Along the way, you may also find some insights about yourself and what you want to achieve. I know that I did.

—**Jenny Macdonald**, Non-Executive Director

Early in my career whilst an employee of a major Australian bank, I asked the CEO at the time 'What makes a great leader?'. He responded with 'Great followers'. As simple as this sounded it is something that resonated with me. Great teams are developed and influenced by authentic and nurturing leaders. Team members follow the leader not because they have to, but because they want to.

In this book, Michelle clearly identifies aspects and traits of what differentiates a good boss from a bad boss. There are some wonderful insights, and 'time outs' which encourage and enable introspection to assist readers to identify what role they can play in assisting a bad boss if they work for one, how they might better influence and coach a bad boss if they manage one, or open their eyes and mindset to understand and determine if they are in fact a bad boss.

Working through this book it became clear to me that through my leadership journey I have found myself in all three situations. If I had access then to the tips and tools in this book, the change required in all instances would have been far easier to navigate. If you are prepared to invest the time and effort to reflect, seek feedback and take action then the outcomes detailed in this book are well within reach.

—**Robert Ford**, Chief Executive Officer,
Victorian Leaders

As our individual relationships to work keep changing, our relationships with the people at work remains key to our well-being and our performance. It's no surprise that for most employees their most important professional relationship is with their boss. Through this deft collection of frameworks and insights, Michelle provides a powerful challenge to take ownership of how we relate to each other on a human level with humility and authenticity. Her personal reflections on how she's refocussed her own approach provides a wonderfully simple message of hope for how we can evolve our relationships in the workplace ... 'I built lasting friendships and connections that enabled us to do more and be more'.

—**Daniel Madhavan**, Chief Executive Officer,
Impact Investment Group

In the corporate world, leaders often feel powerless either working for a bad boss or as an ineffective leader. Michelle's book provides an excellent framework to help navigate a pathway to positively change the situation you may be in, whether you are early in your career or a senior executive.

—**Lynley Corcoran**, HR Executive

Michelle Gibbings is a refreshing voice in a sea of authentic leadership, sharing helpful and practical solutions for both bosses and employees based on her own extensive leadership and coaching experience along with insights from the latest research.

In this book, Michelle makes a compelling case to truly understand the impact an authentic leader can have and offers surprisingly practical questions to generate awareness and actionable steps for both the boss and employee to own their role in cultivating a positive employment relationship.

—**Deborah Greenwood-Smith**, Chief Operating Officer, Equiem

As someone who has been working for over 35 years, I found *Bad Boss* to be very relatable to my experience in the corporate world and sometimes uncomfortable as I recognised examples of my own behaviour when I wasn't at my best. The power of Michelle's book is that she helps make this behaviour discussable and provides practical and implementable strategies for improving the most critical working relationship we have.

—**Steve Whiteling**, Chief Risk Officer

BAD BOSS

BAD BOSS

WHAT TO DO IF YOU WORK FOR ONE, MANAGE ONE OR ARE ONE

MICHELLE GIBBINGS

WILEY

First published in 2020 by John Wiley & Sons Australia, Ltd
42 McDougall St, Milton Qld 4064

Office also in Melbourne

Typeset in Adobe Garamond Pro 11/13pt

ISBN: 978-0-730-38397-0

A catalogue record for this book is available from the National Library of Australia

Cover design: Kathy Davis/Wiley

10 9 8 7 6 5 4 3 2 1

Disclaimer
The material in this publication is of the nature of general comment only, and does not represent professional advice. It is not intended to provide specific guidance for particular circumstances and it should not be relied on as the basis for any decision to take action or not take action on any matter which it covers. Readers should obtain professional advice where appropriate, before making any such decision. To the maximum extent permitted by law, the author and publisher disclaim all responsibility and liability to any person, arising directly or indirectly from any person taking or not taking action based on the information in this publication.

CONTENTS

ABOUT THE AUTHOR

Michelle Gibbings is a workplace expert obsessed with building workplaces where leaders and employees thrive, and great things happen.

She's the author of *Step Up: How to build your influence at work* and *Career Leap: How to reinvent and liberate your career.*

Through her passion and advocacy for better ways of leading and working, Michelle has built a distinguished reputation as the keynote speaker, adviser and executive mentor of choice for leading edge corporates and global organisations.

Before establishing her leadership practice, she worked for some of the world's biggest organisations — much of the time in senior leadership positions. Yes, she's been the employee, boss and boss's boss too.

She regularly appears across a range of media including *The Sydney Morning Herald*, *The Australian*, the *Australian Financial Review*, the *Herald Sun*, *CEO Magazine*, *HR Director*, the *Today* show and various radio stations.

When not facilitating sessions, mentoring, writing or speaking at conferences, Michelle loves to travel and experience life with her best friend and husband, Craig.

Michelle lives in Melbourne, Australia, with Craig and their dog, Barney.

michellegibbings.com

ACKNOWLEDGEMENTS

A book is never written alone. It is the culmination of insights, ideas and inspiration from many sources.

To the many people throughout my career who have shaped my leadership vision and helped me get places I'd never have imagined I could go, thank you! To my clients, who are a constant source of inspiration and connection, I consider myself privileged to work with you. To my brother-in-law, Warwick Parer, who came up with the initial title of this book, thanks for the suggestion.

Thanks to my editor, Kelly Irving, for her amazing work in keeping me on track and to the Wiley team for their continuing support.

Most of all thanks to my husband, Craig Salisbury, who when I announced I was going to write my third book, once again gave me his wholehearted support. I couldn't do this without your love, care and backing.

PREFACE

Fictionalised in movies, but all too real in offices, factories and worksites around the world, we've all worked for one — the bad boss.

They're disorganised or dysfunctional or they can't control their temper. They steal your ideas and rarely if ever acknowledge or appreciate your efforts. Worse still are the bullies who intimidate you and generally make your working life hell.

From Gordon Gecko in *Wall Street* to Mr Burns in *The Simpsons*, a bad boss story makes for good drama and even comedy, but in life it's no fun. It can be downright miserable. You probably remember *The Devil Wears Prada*, in which the main protagonist and horrible boss Miranda Priestly, immortalised on the silver screen by Meryl Streep, torments her long-suffering assistant Andy, played by Anne Hathaway. This story (like so many movies) began life as a book, and at the time I read it, it all felt a little too close to home, because I felt like I was working for a male version of Miranda Priestly, and it was taking a toll on my wellbeing.

> A bad boss makes you dread going to work, impacts your self-esteem and, over time, affects your mental health.

Oddly, though, I wouldn't be where I am now if I hadn't gone through that turbulence. I was fortunate because I had supportive people around me who helped me navigate my way through.

In the end, the role was pivotal in shaping and elevating my career choices. (And it now provides great content and lessons for a book like this!)

Confessions of a bad boss

I've also been privileged to have worked with amazing leaders who set the standard for the type of leader I wanted to be. They challenged how I saw my role as a leader. They inspired me to do better. Leaders are not all, or always, 'bad'. But I do have a confession to make.

You see, I was once one of those horrible bosses.

I didn't yell or scream or throw my handbag or other objects at people (as Miranda did), but I could make life really hard for my team. I was often relentless on expectations and workload, and I kept my team members at a distance. I didn't have enough time for them, nor did I try to get to know them.

When I was promoted into that management role—I'd be stretching the truth to call myself a leader back then—I had no idea what I was doing. I loved the *idea* of being someone others looked to for direction, but I simply wasn't equipped with the leadership skills to actually *be* that someone. I made it up as I went along, with a few hits and many misses.

> Like most people, I didn't deliberately set out to be a bad boss ... I just didn't know any better.

Perfectionism and ambition are a toxic combination. I didn't want to admit to my boss that I couldn't do something or to deliver substandard work, so there was always pressure to perform, and I would set a cracking pace. When the pressure of the work environment got to me, I passed it down the line, so the pressure on team increased too. My team members were exhausted. Sadly, I was blind to this impact.

One day, just after my team and I had come off a massive project, I was sitting at my desk and muttered, half to myself, 'I'm so glad that's done. I'm stuffed.' To which one of my team members responded, 'Thank god there's an off switch.' Surprised, I asked what she meant. She said, 'Your energy levels and drive are so high. Your capacity for work is relentless. It's impossible for us to keep up with you. It's good to see you get tired too.'

In hindsight, I shouldn't have been surprised, yet I was.

Thankfully, with a lot of work and coaching I improved. It didn't happen overnight. It started with an awareness of the impact I was having and a desire to do better, then having people around me who could help me see myself more clearly.

I learned over the years to get explicit with my team about how I work, and to ask for their help to slow me down. I learned that the more open I was with my team about my own limitations and strengths, the more we brought out the best in each other. I also learned that the more the team connected with me on a human level, and I with them, the better we worked together.

I built lasting friendships and connections that enabled us to do more and be more.

Why this book and why now

Since leaving corporate I've worked with hundreds of leaders across the private and public sectors, and at all levels of organisations. What I see time and time again is good people in tough (and even horrible) situations. The most frequent complaint or challenge they confront is their relationship with their boss.

When I talk with the boss, their most frequent complaint or challenge is their relationship with *their* boss, the challenges in the team along with ever tighter deadlines, increasing expectations and unrealistic workloads.

When I talk with the boss's boss, their lament is the rumbles they hear about things not working, and again the challenges of a work environment that is tough (at one end of the spectrum) to toxic (at the other end). Where they face worries on multiple fronts, not least in relation to job security, performance, outcomes and reputation, and also express fears and frustrations about their relationships.

Everyone reports to someone and everyone faces challenges!

> This book isn't a bitch-fest about bastard leaders or a litany of bad boss stories. Rather, it's a book about hope.

The world desperately needs good leaders. Leaders who will challenge the standard orthodoxy of leadership practices in organisations. Leaders who are willing to tackle the big issues we face as humans. Leaders who want to bring out the best in their team because they know that when their team members thrive, everyone benefits.

At the same time, the world needs happy, healthy and engaged workers who bring their whole and best selves to work every day. Workers who do their best and are at their best.

Call me optimistic or naïve, but I don't believe that most people who are classified as 'bad' bosses or leaders intend to be bad (unless, of course, they're a corporate psychopath who takes pleasure in other people's pain and in making their working life a misery, but there aren't so many of those!).

How to use this book

Creating an environment where employees and leaders flourish is a team effort. So regardless of your role — be it employee, boss or leader, boss's boss or leader of leaders — this book encourages you to play your part. It challenges you to critically examine your role in the dynamic, and to own what you can do to shift your relationship and make it work. This is not about settling scores or getting even; it's about moving forward productively and positively. It's about building your awareness, creating and implementing effective strategies, and reflecting on your progress.

No one chooses to be classified as a 'bad boss'. If you're in a role where you work for someone you deem to be one, then you may be tempted to think, 'This is all about them, and not about me.' Not so fast!

Relationships are both an individual and a team effort. Look at any team sport to see how everyone plays a part. Regardless of the role or title you hold, on or off the field, how you behave influences whether that experience is positive or negative. The same applies in the working world.

In this book you'll read real-life stories of employees who have reshaped their situation, bosses who have changed how they lead, and bosses of leaders who have opened their eyes to the role they need to play to build a better culture.

You'll see the good, the bad and the ugly. To protect the innocent the names in the *On the field* stories have been altered. You'll see change is possible, relationships can be improved and there is always choice and hope.

There are things in our work life we may not like (or be proud of), but it's up to us to acknowledge our part, learn from our experiences and be willing to evolve. I hope this book will challenge and guide you to a new way of thinking and being, regardless of your role.

You may be tempted to focus only on the part of the book you feel most resonates with you; however, I highly recommend you first read all three parts.

For example, as an employee, you may not manage other people, so you're tempted to read only Part I. However, you'll find reading about what is going on for your boss, manager or leader in Part III will help you improve your situation.

Or you may find yourself managing an ineffective leader, so you skip to Part II. Yet if you read Part III you may discover that your behaviour is contributing to the poor dynamic, and that without realising it you have become that leader's 'bad boss', which means you will need to do some work on yourself using Part III before you can expect them to change.

To be successful, to come out the other end in a better position than you are in now, you need to understand the challenges and opportunities from all three perspectives.

This means you need to be open to challenging your perspective about what is really going on before you can determine your best approach and take action. That's why you'll be asked regularly to take *Time out* to consider a few pertinent questions as you progress through the book.

So read and reflect, and above all play nice and have a laugh! Sometimes we can be horrified when we hold up a mirror and see clearly how we have been contributing to our own problems. But it's not the end of the world. The fact you're reading this demonstrates that you want to do something to improve your situation.

Making real change takes time, patience and practice, so if you need further help and guidance implementing the actions, there are additional resources to help you at:

michellegibbings.com/resources

Now let's get to work to make your workplace work for you!

INTRODUCTION

First, we need to set the scene of the modern workplace. It's an environment that is constantly shifting on every front—except one. The relationship dynamics that occur across the organisation will be a primary source of either irritation or inspiration.

Organisations are based on relationships, and understanding how they work is crucial if you are to thrive rather than merely survive. All work environments have rules of behaviour and standard operating procedures, although they are usually not set down in print. Sometimes these rules are helpful; at other times they do little more than perpetuate stereotypes and myths.

Before we go any further, let's dig into the reality of today's working world, and set the framework you will use to advance your relationships and position on the field.

When woken by that early-morning alarm at the start of another week, do you jump out of bed and think, 'Hooray, it's Monday!', or do you roll over, hit the snooze button and wish it was Saturday?

Your reaction is in large part determined by the relationships you have at work. You don't need research studies to tell you that you are far more likely to enjoy going to work if you work with people you like and have a positive and healthy relationship with your boss.

Sadly, the reality is that for many of us, our working environment isn't much fun, and in extreme cases can actually be damaging our health.

> You know it's true: People don't leave their job, they leave their boss.

In May 2019, the 194 members of the World Health Organization (WHO) unanimously agreed to amend the International Classification of Diseases and Related Health Problems to classify professional burnout as a recognised illness. The WHO defines professional burnout as 'a syndrome conceptualised as resulting from chronic workplace stress that has not been successfully managed'.

Beyond Blue's landmark 2017 study 'State of Workplace Mental Health in Australia' found that:

- 52 per cent of employees believe their workplace is mentally healthy
- 56 per cent believe their most senior leader values mental health
- 21 per cent had taken time off work in the prior 12 months because they felt stressed, anxious, depressed or mentally unhealthy.

Supporting these findings, a PwC report into the costs of mental health concluded that absenteeism costs Australian businesses about $4.7 billion every year. Presenteeism, where people are less productive in their role due to mental health issues, costs around $6.1 billion a year, and compensation claims cost an estimated $146 million a year.

The employee–boss dynamic also impacts workplace productivity and culture, and ultimately organisational outcomes. The Great Place to Work Institute found that trust between managers and employees is a defining characteristic of organisations listed in their annual '100 Best Companies to Work for' list. Similarly, a study by Alex Edmans, Professor of Finance at the London Business School, found that the top companies to work for increased their share value by 50 per cent.

Regardless of where you sit in the organisational hierarchy, you have a boss (whether a manager, CEO or Board), and your relationship with them impacts your productivity, satisfaction levels, wellbeing and career prospects either positively or negatively.

So it's in everyone's best interests for relationships at work to, well, work.

Why is this easier said than done?

The leadership deficit

Search the business archives and read the business press and you'll find a long litany of organisations—think Tyco, Enron, HIH, James Hardie, WorldCom, Satyam and more—that eventually self-destructed because of toxic leadership and unethical cultures. In Australia, the Financial Services Royal Commission, established in late 2017, uncovered many examples of questionable corporate practices.

We are passing through a period of history the World Economic Forum has dubbed 'the Fourth Industrial Revolution'. Leaders and bosses are urged to experiment with products, solutions and new ways of working, as well as to manage complex, interconnected systems and multiple needs, all the while motivating employees, peers and other stakeholders, and working long hours and feeling insecure about their own jobs. (Phew!)

It's little wonder that some bosses don't make the grade, or that so many workplaces around the world are neither happy nor healthy.

Here are some more revealing statistics—and be warned, they're more than a little depressing.

Gallup reported in 2017 that 82 per cent of employees find their leaders uninspiring, only 15 per cent of employees are engaged at work, and only one in three employees strongly agree that they trust the leadership of their organisation.

Research in Australia by the University of Wollongong found half of all employees will experience workplace bullying (including verbal abuse, humiliation, social isolation, withholding information and spreading rumours) during their careers. Of those bullied, 40 per cent experienced workplace bullying early in their career and between 5 and 7 per cent had been bullied in the previous six months. Young males with limited social support at work and those who worked in stressful environments were found to be most at risk.

And if that isn't enough …

In 2012, a US survey found 65 per cent of Americans said getting rid of their boss would make them happier than getting a pay rise. A UK study found 40 per cent of survey participants didn't think their boss was good at their job, a third thought they could perform better than their manager, and a fifth said their manager was the single worst thing about their job. Another British study reported similar sentiments, with two-fifths of respondents saying their manager didn't improve morale at work, while one in three felt uncomfortable approaching their boss for help.

Of course, when we have a crap day, that crap day usually follows us home … so our home life suffers, along with our relationships and wellbeing. When the pressure gets too much, people become alienated and numb; they search for crutches, drinking too much, eating badly, turning to substance abuse or other unhealthy behaviours to get them through.

People spend up to a third of their waking hours at work, so if they are working in an environment that impacts their health and wellbeing this has flow-on effects for the wider community.

Today we face huge problems of social isolation and dislocation, which are sadly evidenced by the growing rise of mental health issues and suicide. While toxic workplaces aren't the sole cause, there's no doubt they are a contributory factor.

> When employees are stressed out, when leaders are leading badly and when workplace cultures are toxic, everyone suffers.

Good leadership matters to all of us

Now, before you toss this book aside in despair, the good news is it's not all doom and gloom. This dire situation can absolutely be reversed!

In a nutshell, *better bosses = happier and more engaged employees = happier and healthier workplaces = better performance (individually and collectively).*

When I'm working with groups to improve team dynamics, one of the exercises I often get them to do is reflect on a time when they worked in a high-performing team. In fact, you can try this now.

How many examples can you think of? Often people can recall only one or two times in their professional life, and a handful of people can only think of examples from their personal life, but I've yet to find someone who can't think of any such time at all. That's important here, because it shows we all know what it feels like to work in a great environment.

It's likely you remembered a time that made you feel good. When you were at your best. When you achieved something great or felt valued for your contribution. When you liked your team, you worked well together and you had a great leader.

When you are happy, you get more done. You're more focused and committed to your work, which means fewer mistakes and better outcomes. The work environment is more stable, there's less turnover and sick leave, less conflict and fewer behavioural challenges. When you're happy, you are more creative and effective at solving problems. You are more resilient, better able to bounce back and deal with setbacks and conflict, even when what you are working on is challenging and complex.

For leaders of those teams, life is easier and more enjoyable. Less time is spent cleaning up messes. There is nothing more fulfilling for a leader than working with people to help them achieve their goals and to progress.

With rare exceptions, most people in leadership roles *want* to be a good leader.

Why would they not?

Eight myths of the modern workplace

Before we get into exploring the dynamics of the work environment, how they impact us and what we can do about it, we first have to bust some assumptions we currently hold about what good leadership is and isn't, and how this affects the entire workplace.

Myth 1: Leadership is a title

We often have a narrow view of what a leader is because we see leaders defined by hierarchical positions and the level of positional power they hold.

I prefer a more expansive and inclusive approach to leadership, where each of us can play a role should we choose to step up to the plate. I like the definition posed by marketing expert and prolific blogger Seth Godin: 'Leaders create the conditions where people choose new actions. The choices are voluntary. They're made by people who see a new landscape, new opportunities and new options. You can't make people change. But you can create an environment where they choose to.'

In a similar vein, researcher and author Dr Brené Brown defines a leader as 'anyone who takes responsibility for finding the potential in people and processes, and who has the courage to develop that potential'.

To me, leaders are people who help shape where we want to get to and align people to make that happen, and they do this in a way that brings out the best in everyone involved, so all contribute to the best of their ability and are valued in the process.

Leadership is not about your title or the positional power you hold; it's about the role you play.

This means having people reporting to you makes you a manager or a boss, but it doesn't automatically make you a leader!

Myth 2: Leading is a one-size-fits-all approach

During my time in corporate, I saw amazing leaders step up with courage, and lead with good intent. They made tough decisions when necessary, put the needs of the team before their own and actively developed each team member to be their best and to get to where they wanted to get to. Yet each of these leaders led differently.

Everyone wants and deserves to be treated with respect and dignity, but beyond that there are differences. Some people like leaders who are strategic; others prefer them to be more directive; still others would have them be more laissez-faire, for example. We are all unique individuals, with varying experiences, cultures, skill levels, personality traits, and levels of self-awareness and self-actualisation. Consequently, what motivates you will probably be different from what I (or your colleagues) like and respond to.

Leadership is also contextual, and with different environments and challenges different strategies are needed to bring out the best in people. That's why we must keep an open mind as we head further into this book.

Different people thrive under different types of leadership.

Myth 3: Leaders are not needed in a flat organisational structure

One recent management theory posits that the role of the 'manager' and 'leader' is disappearing. The argument is that as organisations move to flatter structures and more agile ways of working, the need for dedicated managers or leaders is receding.

Harvard professor Ethan Bernstein and colleagues write, 'In self-managed organisations, leadership is distributed among roles, not individuals (people usually hold multiple roles, on various teams). Leadership responsibilities continually shift as the work changes and as teams create and define new roles.'

This creates a more fluid environment for leadership, certainly. But even with this fluidity there's still, more often than not, some hierarchy, process, decision criteria, performance reviews and rules around who gets to do what. You are still going to be reporting to someone, somewhere.

Another way of looking at it is that if you no longer rely on rules and structures to get things done, you need to rely on connection, influence and purpose instead. To succeed you need all the players knowing the game plan and playing their part, not running onto the field blissfully unaware of what their teammates are doing.

Consequently, while in this new world of work who you work for and with will change constantly, the need for clear accountability, strong team dynamics, personal connection and healthy relationships will persist.

Less structure and hierarchy and more self-management creates a need for *more*, not *less*, emphasis on leadership and healthy working relationships.

Myth 4: Leadership is an innate ability

Very few bosses will have the humility to suggest they acquired their leadership position through luck. Generally they'll attribute it to hard work, intellect and a raft of other skills.

In many cases they'll have all that and more, but if you come from a certain background and exhibit certain character traits you are more likely to rise to the top. This includes being seen as an extrovert, confident, self-assured, dynamic and decisive.

Analysis by Professor Timothy Judge from the University of Notre Dame of the 'Big Five' personality traits (openness, agreeableness, conscientiousness, extroversion and neuroticism) found that extroversion followed by conscientiousness were the best predictors of leadership. Agreeableness was the weakest.

Psychologist and decision-making expert Daniel Kahneman found there is a strong expectation that leaders will be decisive and act quickly. He wrote, 'We deeply want to be led by people who know what they're doing and who don't have to think about it too much.'

When we look at the statistics on leadership roles and diversity across all categories, including age, ethnicity, gender and background, we often find a great deal of conformity. However, a person who exhibits certain personality traits isn't by default a good or bad leader. A person may be born with natural traits that make becoming a boss easier, but being a good leader is a skill that can be learned.

If you are working for a bad boss, if you yourself are a bad boss or if you have a bad boss in your team, the good news is change is possible.

Leadership is a learned skill.

Myth 5: Leaders have no emotions

We say we want leaders who share who they are and how they feel, yet we don't want them to overshare or be too vulnerable. We say we want nurturing work cultures where everyone can express their feelings and bring their authentic self to work, yet we get uncomfortable if we see people at work crying or being too emotional. We expect leaders to be in control so we can step away from connecting, because we would rather avoid the emotional and difficult conversation. Talk about a tough audience to please!

To succeed at work — to build strong, healthy relationships — you have to harness and leverage your emotions. There's no way around it. Remember, we are human. To be human is to be emotional, because relationships and connections can't be created without feelings.

> Being an effective leader and employee is about connecting, and you can't connect without emotions and feelings.

Myth 6: Bad leadership is attributable to bad people

We believe we are accurate assessors of other people — who they are, their intent and beliefs, their abilities and what they think of us. And we think we are brilliant assessors of ourselves.

In truth, we're not.

We all have ingrained patterns of thinking and behaving that we have cultivated over the years through our experiences. These experiences create assumptions and expectations about how things should be, and who we are.

This plays out in the expectations we have of our team members, peers and boss, and our disappointment when they don't meet those expectations. The challenge is that our expectations may not match the other person's expectations, and this can lead to conflict and confusion.

Every one of us likes to see ourselves as a good person, yet, as psychological studies such as the Milgram and Stanford Prison experiments, and countless real-world events, have demonstrated, we all possess the ability to dehumanise others. We quickly sort people into 'us' and 'them' and we naturally gravitate towards those we see as 'like us', because it makes us feel more comfortable.

Consequently, when a relationship at work is challenging or breaks down, we can be quick to judge and cast blame on the other party, particularly the so-called 'bad' boss. Yet it's always more complicated than that and each party to the relationship plays a role in shaping the dynamic.

It's often about *us*, as well as about *them*.

Myth 7: Leadership needs are different for different ages

When IBM conducted research across the three primary generations in the workforce today, they found Millennials, Gen X and baby boomers are largely motivated by similar factors: inspirational leadership, a clearly articulated business strategy and performance-based recognition and promotions. The study found that Millennials placed less emphasis on a collaborative work environment, the freedom to innovate and the flexibility to manage their work–life balance than Gen X employees, but overall the differences were small.

It's all too easy to generalise and to say a particular generation will respond best to a specific leadership style. Be cautious about assumptions that a person in a certain age demographic will want to be led (or to lead) in a certain way, or will demonstrate a distinctive behavioural pattern.

Fixed, stereotypical views get in the way of effective communication and relationship building — at any age!

For example, if a Millennial leader holds a fixed mindset that their baby boomer employee is too old to learn and innovate, this will impact their willingness to spend time and energy training them and what type of initiatives they delegate to them.

The solution is to get curious, get interested and find out what makes your work colleagues tick at a personal level — not a stereotypical one.

Myth 8: Leaders, employees and bosses should love their job, no matter what

In today's culture of self-advancement and self-promotion we've manufactured a vision of the idealised workplace, perfect boss and awesome job. We're coerced into believing we should love our job, no matter what our role, follow our dreams and find our passion. And if we don't, we are living a smaller, more circumscribed life.

It's never that simple. As I discussed in my previous book, *Career Leap: How to reinvent and liberate your career*, it's more important to find your purpose. When you know your why and put that at the centre of your decision making, it's easier to make the powerful, wise and congruent choices that serve not just you and the ones you love, but others too.

It's unrealistic to believe that you can or should love every minute of your job—whether you're an employee, a leader or the boss of a leader, or have any other title. It doesn't work like that. This doesn't mean you should stay in a workplace where you are victimised, bullied, humiliated, and made to feel worthless and less than who you are. Happiness at work isn't an oxymoron. You can and should strive for that.

Remember as you keep reading, it's not possible to find happiness in every second of your working life, but it is possible to make choices that will help you like it more, as you'll soon see.

Four steps to freedom and fulfilment

If you've ever been to Yellowstone National Park in the United States, you'll know that the geysers are one of the key attractions—a spectacular feat of nature, where huge volumes of steam constantly erupt out of the ground. It's a great example of pressure at play.

At the surface, there's a caprock, which traps water. In the subsurface there are fissures in the rock, so the water can flow and collect in those cavities. Below that, there's intense heat, which triggers a chain reaction: the water below the surface is heated, eventually boiling and turning into steam, which releases pressure on the water just below it, which in turn boils, creating huge volumes of steam that erupt out of the geyser.

The geysers are part of a system in which constant pressure causes a reaction—up and out. You can't see the pressure; you see only its impact. This natural environmental phenomenon is a system, just as an organisation is.

In organisations, people are linked via relationships, chains of command, work processes, roles, decisions and accountabilities, creating an interconnected and interdependent system.

Bosses don't work in isolation. Employees don't work in isolation. These connections, and how the pressures and expectations are felt, experienced and managed, filter through the system. The actions of one person in the system will impact and produce outcomes — positive or negative — on others in the system. These flow-on impacts softly ripple or crash with seismic impact, depending on their force. The more you push down the system, the more that force will come back at you!

Just as in nature, the actions you take at work are never inconsequential. They will come back at you — in either a good or an unpleasant way.

There are many times, however, when the elements of the chain reaction are shielded from view. What you will see and feel are the impacts, depending on your role and how directly the pressure is applied on you.

Let me explain.

The leadership pressure chamber

The day-to-day work environment often feels like a pressure chamber, doesn't it? Actions and reactions are constantly at play, back and forth, and up and down the organisational hierarchy. When everything is going smoothly and in balance, the work hums along. When the pressure gets too much and things get out of balance, that's when the bubbles turn into blowouts and explosions that impact everyone! No one's perfect and when pressure is applied and the stakes are high, cracks will start to appear.

I once worked on a large-scale change program. The stakes were very high, with big dollars, big expectations, big challenges and big workloads. It was a great team to work in — very collegiate and supportive — but when the pressure was applied from above and politics came into play, it got messy, volatile even.

We set up a series of meetings and presentations for the senior executive team to determine the next phase and the ultimate life of the project. If we didn't get the funding the project would stall or stop, and people would lose their jobs. The pressure to perform was intense. Over this period we waited, somewhat anxiously, to hear the outcomes from the committee meeting where the project's fate was being decided.

On the first round, the outcome wasn't good, which created enormous tension at the leadership level. We'd prepared and worked hard but hadn't secured what we needed. This put pressure on us both as a leadership team and as individual leaders, some of which was inevitably passed on to our team members as we scrambled to re-form, re-prepare and re-diagnose the approach and put forward alternative solutions in a very short space of time. We had incredibly tight timeframes in which to go back to the committee for a second, third and ultimately fourth time. This meant long days, short fuses, stress and occasions when we weren't at our best.

This was a high-functioning team with some fantastic and highly evolved leaders, yet there were days when good leadership was conspicuously not demonstrated. What we did have, though, was good awareness and effective support mechanisms to cushion the impact and ensure our team members were looked after.

> The simple reality is you can't eradicate pressure from the system, so you have to make sure you have the right strategies in place to manage it.

External versus internal demands

Pressures on teams have external and internal sources:

- **External** — customers, environment, political, legislative and regulatory, societal, technological and economic
- **Internal** — executive team/board, cost pressures, mergers, downsizing, new opportunities, demands for increased revenue, strategic reviews and cultural shifts.

Those expectations and demands, regardless of their source, are passed down the organisational food chain from boss's boss to boss to employee. How they are passed down, and the reaction that comes back up the line, depends on the level of pressure applied — how hard, how fast, what type of pressure, its frequency and the nature of the person applying the pressure.

If it's passed down in such a way that the person on the receiving end is receptive, prepared and well positioned to cope with the pressure, then it will be managed well. When that person subsequently passes on the expectations to their team members and they too are similarly prepared, then the impact is largely positive and outcomes progress positively.

This is because the release valve to manage the pressure, which may involve awareness, support, strong team dynamics, a collegiate environment, a good working relationship with the boss and so on, is working well.

This looks like figure I.1.

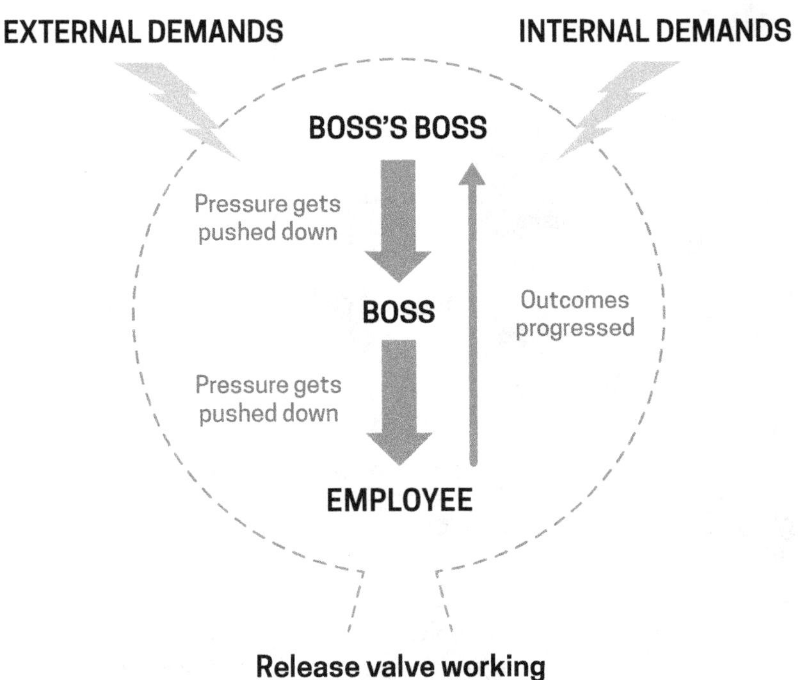

Figure I.1: release valve working

By contrast, if the expectations and demands are passed down badly, and the person receiving is ill-prepared, ill-equipped, unsupported and unable to handle it well, then the result is a chain reaction of negativity. That person, likely a boss, pushes those expectations down to their team, who don't feel supported, and in a challenging environment the pressure builds, ructions in the team start to fissure and the tension eventually boils to the surface. This gets pushed back up the line through increased turnover, reduced productivity, poor engagement and disgruntled employees.

The release valve is broken, faulty or in some cases missing, as illustrated in figure I.2.

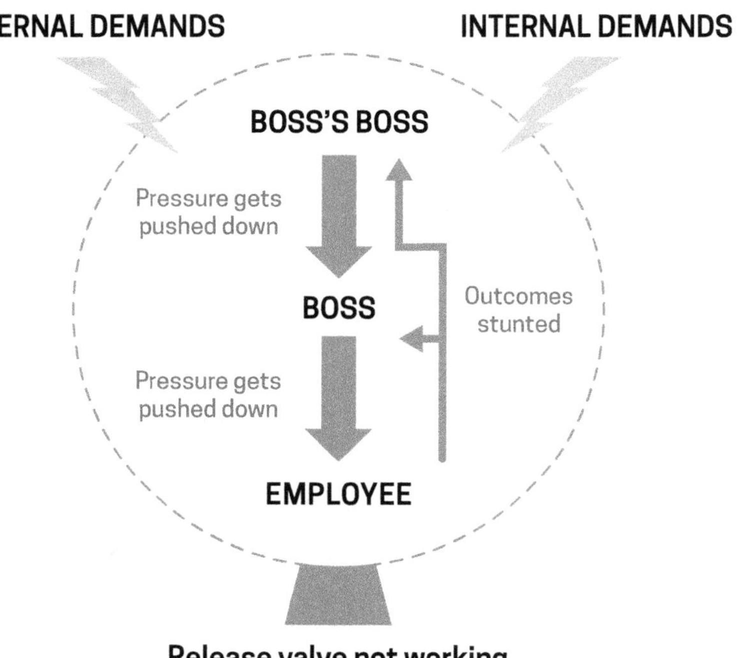

Figure I.2: release valve not working

These positive and negative chain reactions don't happen in isolation, because individuals don't work in a bubble. In any organisation they work in a connected and interdependent system, where actions in one team or division trickle through or explode into other areas, with consequential impacts and effects. This is especially so in environments where there are multiple handovers, joint stakeholders, shared accountability, and dual reporting lines and dependencies.

> Too much pressure in the system, from multiple sources and in multiple teams, will create friction, fractures and fissures.

This creates a workplace that is at best unpleasant and at worst toxic, as figure I.3 illustrates.

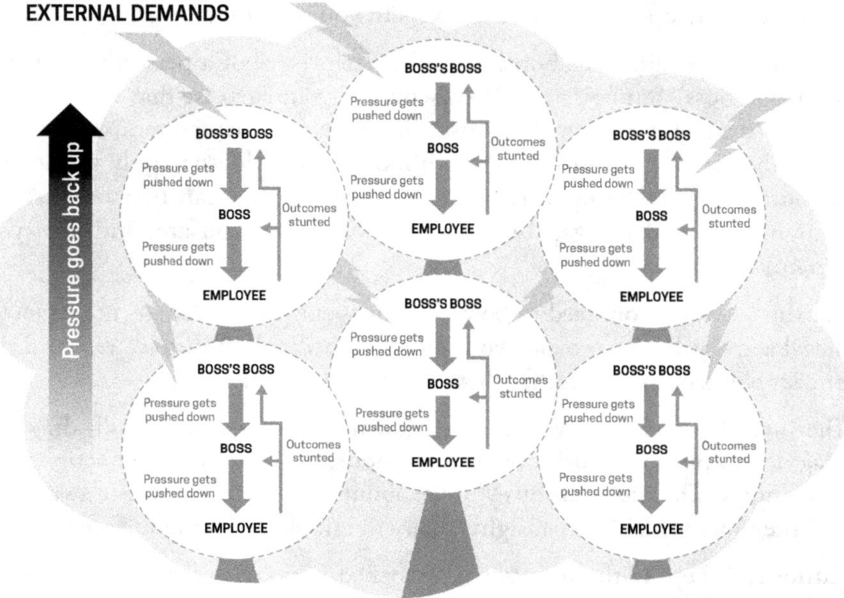

Figure I.3: the toxic workplace

It can be easy to point the finger and say it's all *their* doing, so we need to fix *them*, change *them*, fire *them*, but in a system it's usually never just one person's fault, which is why finding the release valve involves assessing, strategising, acting and reflecting at all levels of the organisational food chain.

You need to understand the whole to be able to figure out your part in it and what you can do to make work work *for* you, not *against* you.

Who eats who?

The solution to easing this pressure is multi-layered. It requires all parties involved to play a role, which is precisely what this book will explore.

First you need to understand that there are three key relationship layers involved. Regardless of the terminology you use in your organisation, they are:

1. the employee
2. the boss or leader
3. the boss's boss or leader of leaders.

Now, you may operate at all three layers in your organisation.

You may be reading this book from the perspective of a person who works for a 'bad boss', but you may also discover to your surprise that for someone in your team, *you're* their 'bad boss'! So while you may be tempted to skip through certain parts of this book thinking, 'That doesn't apply to me', I'd encourage you to be open to all perspectives so you can best understand your impact, and the gap between how you *think* you are, and how you *actually* are.

For this to work, you need to be your own agent provocateur — not to incite illegal activity, but to provoke yourself to really dig deep into ... *you*, and the impact you have on yourself, others and the situation.

The interplay of these levels and relationships involves push–pull, drag up, drag down, push up, push down; the actions, reactions and interactions can be complex. The more curious you are about this, the greater your awareness and the more valuable the insights that will bubble up to the surface.

Curiosity is key. Without it, you'll be locked in your own pressure chamber with an ineffective release valve. As Sir Isaac Newton said, 'What we know is a drop, what we don't know is an ocean.'

> Be ready to suspend judgement, dig deep and get curious about what is and what could be.

Operating the release valve

The release valve has four key phases, applied to each of the three relationship levels identified. These four phases are shown in figure I.4.

- **Phase 1: ASSESS**
  The starting point for every position and role in an organisation is to assess what is going on, what impact it has on you and what may be its cause. You'll be asked to consider: is it them, is it me or is it the environment? (You'll likely find it's a combination of all three, but more on that soon.)
- **Phase 2: STRATEGISE**
  Next, you'll consider and work through your options to determine the best strategic move given the circumstances and the role you are playing in the relationship. This will help you consider actionable approaches and steps to take.

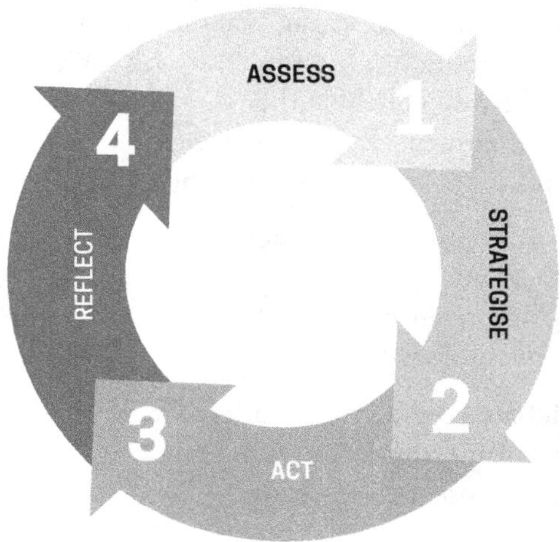

Figure I.4: the four phases to operating the release valve

- **Phase 3: ACT**
  Here you begin to implement your chosen approach, all the while making sure you are taking care of your own wellbeing and that of those around you who are affected. This includes being fair and intentional, living according to your values and, when needed, being courageous.
- **Phase 4: REFLECT**
  In this final phase you will reflect on your progress (or lack of it) and determine any next steps, especially if things are not going according to plan.

Looking at the solution like this appears very linear. Life and work aren't linear, however. In fact, these cycles will likely operate in short bursts and you may find much of the activity runs in parallel.

It can be easy to jump in and think we have very accurately assessed what's happening and why, and therefore what we should do. Often our first impression and interpretation will be wrong, for two reasons:

1. When something happens we immediately think negatively. Our brain is much more predisposed to negative interpretations than positive ones. We catastrophise and overanalyse all too easily, which causes us to be reactive and make moves that could cost us later.

2. We think that what is happening is about us, when in fact it often has nothing to do with us. We interpret 'no' as a slight. When someone fails to say 'hello', we conclude they don't like us. If we see people gossiping in the corner, we are convinced it is about us. It's easy to make assumptions based on little evidence.

Hence, a key part of success is to go slow. Think with your head, heart and gut. Think. Pause. Think again. Reflect, and only then act. This involves conscious thinking and open-hearted reflecting. It's digging deep and getting comfortable being uncomfortable.

This is an approach based on understanding, empathy and compassion, rather than on judgement, blame and loathing. It's facing up to what *you* need to do first, before asking someone else to change.

Regardless of your role, now's your time to challenge yourself to discover an elevated way of thinking, becoming and, ultimately, being. Let the work of you bringing your whole and best self to work begin!

PART I

What to do if you ... WORK FOR ONE

I once worked for someone who was super lovely. He was kind, generous and very supportive. However, he was off-the-chart disorganised. His office was buried under piles of papers, folders, books and an overflowing desk inbox, which is what caused me the most distress in my role.

It was before the days of email (ha, yes, I really am that old!). Items would pour in, but nothing would go out. Memos and requests would get lost; very little was actioned or delegated. Due dates would come and go… and go. Then the phone calls from executives would start: *Where's that report? How come we don't have this data yet?*

Those urgent requests, which needed to be turned around in a day, would then land on my desk. So my day would be one long panic as I rushed around collecting whatever was needed. Of course, those details had to come from other people in the organisation, so I would have to disrupt their day in order to get the material together. I felt the impact because *I* looked disorganised, and I was worried about how that would dent my reputation.

One time when my boss went away on vacation, he asked me to manage his inbox. This was awesome, because then I had ample notice of what was due. When he came back, I just kept that process going. I pretty much took over his inbox, and each day I'd look at what would come in and work out what I needed to do and what I'd leave with him.

Now, you could argue that wasn't my responsibility—and it wasn't. But I couldn't change his operating style. What I could do was change mine to make the situation work for me.

The problem you face may not be so simple to solve. What is common, though, is that you have a choice either to hope your boss will change or to step up and find a way to make it work for you.

> You play a huge role in solving the problem.

This is your career. It's your choice about what you do and don't do. The fact that you've picked up this book shows you want to find a way forward. That's what the following chapters will help you do.

1 ASSESS YOUR POSITION

The cult HBO historical drama *Chernobyl* lays out the catastrophic sequence of events that led to the nuclear disaster at the Chernobyl nuclear power plant in Ukraine in 1986. In the series, the deputy chief engineer, Anatoly Dyatlov, who supervised the test at the plant that ultimately set off the chain reaction, is cast as one of the main villains, along with his two superiors.

The power plant is scheduled to carry out a safety test, which has already been delayed by 10 hours. Dyatlov is impatient because of the expectations of the more senior plant officials, including plant director Viktor Bryukhanov and chief engineer Nikolai Fomin. It's now late in the evening. The shift has changed and it is well past midnight. The control board technicians, one of whom is inexperienced and is being coached through the process by his supervisor, are ordered by Dyatlov to carry out the test, despite it breaching standard protocols.

In the show, Dyatlov is seen yelling at the team, berating them for their stupidity, threatening them and rebuffing their concerns when they suggest aborting the test. The test is carried out, the reactor stalls and experiences a massive power spike, and when the emergency shutdown process is activated a design flaw in the reactor's control rods spikes the power further—and the reactor explodes.

Apparently the writers took some creative licence in the portrayal of certain characters, but the drama offers a powerfully graphic illustration of the damage caused by toxic bosses who yell, belittle, bully and don't listen.

Those toxic bosses, however, were also working in an environment where failure to deliver had real consequences for them, and not good ones, which was very likely to have influenced their decisions. That doesn't excuse their behaviour, but it does help explain it.

It's very easy to classify and box people as good or bad, hero or villain, victim or culprit. It makes us feel good. It can also absolve us of our responsibility for what happens. But reality is never that one-sided or simple. Life is complex. People are complex. And they are rarely all bad. Clinically diagnosed workplace sociopaths or psychopaths are uncommon.

There are at least two sides to every story!

Fact versus fiction

When you get home from work and walk in the door and your housemate or partner asks, 'How was your day?' do you launch into a long commentary on what your boss said or didn't say, or what they should or shouldn't have done?

Perhaps they didn't give you credit for your work, or they stole your idea, telling their boss it was their own. You may feel your efforts are ignored or unappreciated. Maybe you saw them lavishing attention and rewards on the team member you believe is their 'favourite'. Or you've spent hours working on a report that has garnered you only unfavourable feedback. And they've just sent you an email with an urgent and long to-do list with no consideration of your already heavy workload. You feel like they are setting you up to fail or are creating a toxic environment in which you are being pitted against other team members. Or they've simply stuffed up and you feel you are being left to clean up their mess.

Whatever the situation or trigger, after their actions comes your interpretation of them. You'll ponder and deliberate, over and over:

- why they said it
- why they did it
- what it means for you
- how it demonstrates what they think of you
- what it means for how you see them and your relationship with them
- how unfair, unhelpful and typical it was of them
- how it just reinforced why they are a bad boss.

Perhaps you have judged your boss to be ineffective, unethical, power-hungry, a bully, a narcissist, a perfectionist, a micro-managing control freak, or some other not so nice word that defines how you see them.

They may be all that and more, or perhaps there's more to it than this.

What is fact and what is fiction is in the eye of the beholder. You'll have your interpretation of what's playing out, and your boss is likely to see things differently. The truth will usually lie somewhere in the middle.

Own your impact

Finding that middle ground starts with looking into YOU. Now you may be thinking, 'Damn, I was hoping I could blame them — it would make it so much easier.' Sorry, you have to understand, challenge, accept and likely adjust your part to make this dynamic work. It's almost impossible to assess a situation accurately if you don't understand the part you are playing in what's happening.

Are you really bringing your best self to work every day?

The answer may well be 'yes', or it could be a 'maybe', a 'don't know' or a 'no'. When situations at work aren't working, it could be that you are in the wrong role or that your boss or organisation isn't bringing out the best in you. This doesn't make you a bad person.

But perhaps your work habits are less than ideal and are impacting your productivity, working relationships and reputation, and ultimately how your boss treats you. You have to be honest with yourself, especially when it comes to your performance and behaviour.

Poor habits can strain working relationships and ultimately stretch them to breaking point.

Let's take a closer look.

Are you firing on all cylinders?

Downtime and holidays are essential for your mental health and wellbeing. This is when you get the chance to reconnect with friends and family, and to reflect on life, where you are going and what you want to do next.

Mini breaks are great, but longer breaks (beyond a week) are much better at providing time to rest, recharge and reflect. As well, if you frequently burn the candle at both ends—working late, taking work home and always working weekends—you will eventually burn out.

When you aren't in good shape, your work suffers, as does your ability to handle stressful and demanding situations.

Are you getting enough sleep?

When your brain is tired you tend to take the path of least resistance, letting past expectations and assumptions drive your thoughts and actions, and you'll decide the way you've always decided.

Dealing with work pressure is easier when you're well rested. You'll then be far better equipped to step into courageous conversations with your boss, manage a heavy workload and make well-reasoned decisions.

Are you a meeting junkie?

When you rush from meeting to meeting or event to event, you can get to the end of the day exhausted yet having achieved little on your to-do list.

It's important to structure your day so you get the most important things done first. Allow time for regular breaks, during which you get away from your desk for at least 30 minutes. When you change your environment, you change your state, making it likely that the problem you were trying to solve becomes easier to resolve.

As well, having daily intentions and a prioritised work schedule helps you stay on track, better enabling you to meet the commitments you've made to your boss.

Are you always late?

When you keep people waiting you are effectively saying, 'My time is more important than yours', unconsciously implying that you regard yourself as more important. When you miss deadlines, you show yourself to be unreliable and difficult to work with. A regular pattern of tardiness does nothing to enhance your reputation. This includes being the person who constantly misses deadlines, letting your boss and colleagues down.

Are you setting the bar too high?

We are often told we need to set goals, but not just any goals—BIG GOALS. Remember the 'BHAG' acronym, for 'big, hairy, audacious goals'? Yet research shows that setting goals that are too high and too hard actually inhibits progress. You are far more likely to progress when you break it down into bite-size, manageable chunks.

It's great to be ambitious and set stretch targets, but what's more important to a boss is reliability and consistently good performance.

Do you avoid saying 'no'?

There's nothing worse than feeling like you are drowning in work and yet are unappreciated as more and more work comes your way. It's very easy to say 'yes' when a request comes in, yet there will be times when you need to say 'no'.

It helps to set realistic boundaries around what you will and won't do, and how you will respond to requests outside standard working hours. If you don't set boundaries that you are comfortable with, you'll ultimately end up resenting your boss.

Are you the office energy thief?

An energy thief saps you of energy, drains your focus, wastes your time and can throw you off track.

Energy thieves focus on their needs, showing little or no interest in those of other people. They constantly focus on the negative, seeking to drag others down with them. They expect people to do things for them, demanding attention and support, yet are not prepared to offer the same support to others.

Being seen as political, a gossip or an energy thief will do nothing to endear you to your boss, who may classify you as the 'problem child', making it harder to form a healthy and constructive relationship with them.

How many of these habits are you sometimes, or often, guilty of?

TIME OUT

Are you firing on all cylinders?

- Are you taking time out to rest and recharge?
- If not, how is this impacting your work performance and your relationship with your boss?

Are you getting enough sleep?

- Is a lack of sleep impacting your work performance?
- If so, in what ways is this impacting your relationship with your boss?

Are you a meeting junkie?

- Is a lack of prioritisation affecting your work performance?
- If so, how is this impacting your relationship with your boss?

Are you always late?

- Do you frequently miss or push out deadlines?
- If so, are you letting your boss down?

Are you setting the bar too high?

- Are you setting yourself up for success by setting realistic goals?
- Are you over-promising, but under-delivering?
- If so, how is this influencing your boss's perspective on your work performance?

Do you avoid saying 'no'?

- Is your eagerness to please or fear of saying 'no' impacting your work performance?
- Do you have agreed boundaries with your boss in relation to working hours?

Are you the office energy thief?

- Do you get caught up in office politics and bring negative energy into the workplace, affecting how you work with people?
- If so, how is this impacting your boss's perspective of you?

Put yourself in their shoes

Many years ago, I worked with a person who had a warped view of her own performance. She was diligent and kind, but she had a major blind spot: a complete unwillingness to see she could ever improve what she did. She thought everything she did was awesome.

Being her leader was really hard. If I gave any negative feedback in a performance conversation she would dissolve into tears. The problem was she was in a highly technical role and not good at key parts of her job, so I had to provide that feedback.

> To be your best at work, you have to be prepared to dig deep into how you think you are and how you actually are.

That's hard, and it can hurt. However, it is the only way to move forward and improve. After doing this, you may find that the shift you need to make is only small, or it may be large. But at least you know where you stand, and with that self-awareness you can start making the changes necessary to position yourself well to progress.

Put yourself in your boss's shoes for a minute and consider whether you would be easy or hard to work with. Table 1.1 can help you with this exercise.

Table 1.1: hard or easy to work with

THE DIFFICULT EMPLOYEE (HARD TO WORK WITH)	**THE EXEMPLARY EMPLOYEE (EASY TO WORK WITH)**
Do you: • do the least amount of work possible? • regularly deliver below expectations? • think the relationship is all about what you need? • think it's solely your boss's responsibility to make the relationship work?	Do you: • always try your best? • deliver on expectations? • strive to build healthy and constructive working relationships with colleagues? • recognise relationships are a two-way street and you play a part in making the relationship with your boss work?
You are bringing less than your best to work.	*You are bringing your best self to work.*

Are you the sort of team member you would hire, or do you need to improve?

Challenge yourself

Of course, there may be legitimate reasons for your poor work performance. Perhaps your boss has been driving you so hard you've reached breaking point. Perhaps you've tried to turn the relationship around, and nothing seems to change, so over time your productivity and self-esteem have taken a hit. Yes, your boss has their own story to tell too!

Over the years, the most common complaints I receive from people about their boss is that they don't:

- appreciate me or back me enough
- invest enough in my development or help me progress my career
- act consistently or treat people equally
- work hard enough, expecting me to work harder than them
- behave professionally, often being rude and unfriendly
- create a strong sense of a team.

Curiously, what we find most annoying and frustrating about other people is often exactly what we do to others and ourselves.

So how would you rate yourself against those same statements? Let's do a check using table 1.2.

Table 1.2: a self-check

COMPLAINT ABOUT BOSS	CHALLENGE YOUR CONSISTENCY (DO YOU ...)	SELF-ASSESSMENT (YES / NO)
They don't appreciate me.	Appreciate and congratulate yourself when you've done well?	

They don't back me enough.	Have the courage to back yourself by having the difficult conversations with your boss, saying no when you need to and asking for what you need?	
They don't invest enough in my development.	Set aside time and resources each year to support your growth and development?	
They don't help me progress my career.	See yourself as the leader of your career and take proactive steps to enhance both your career and, over time, your life?	
They are inconsistent.	Have focus and direction, stick to goals you've set and deliver on commitments, despite the challenges and setbacks?	
They don't treat people equally.	Treat yourself as well as you treat other people, finding time to meet your needs?	
They expect me to work harder than them.	Place realistic expectations on yourself or others about what can get done and by when?	
They are rude and unfriendly, and make me feel excluded.	Treat all people with fairness and dignity, seeking to understand their needs and what is going on for them, and to make them feel included?	

If you found yourself typically answering in the negative, then you have some work to do to align your behaviour with your own expectations.

Answering these questions isn't easy, so it can help to run your answers past a buddy, colleague or mentor who may help you see a different perspective.

Assess your boss's style

Now you've assessed the part you are playing, you can start to assess your boss'.

In one study Nathan Brooks, a forensic psychologist, found that 21 per cent of corporate leaders demonstrated 'clinically significant' psychopathic traits. 'Typically,' he observed, 'psychopaths create a lot of chaos and generally tend to play people off against each other ... For psychopaths, it is a game and they don't mind if they violate morals. It is about getting where they want in the company and having dominance over others.'

From my experience, bad bosses are usually out of their depth and struggling with a toxic environment that doesn't bring out their best.

> So before you rush to pass judgement and sentence on your boss, it pays to understand what drives them and their behaviour.

Over my working life, I've come across four types of bosses (see figure 1.1). How they operate depends on their awareness of their impact, and the degree to which they care about that impact.

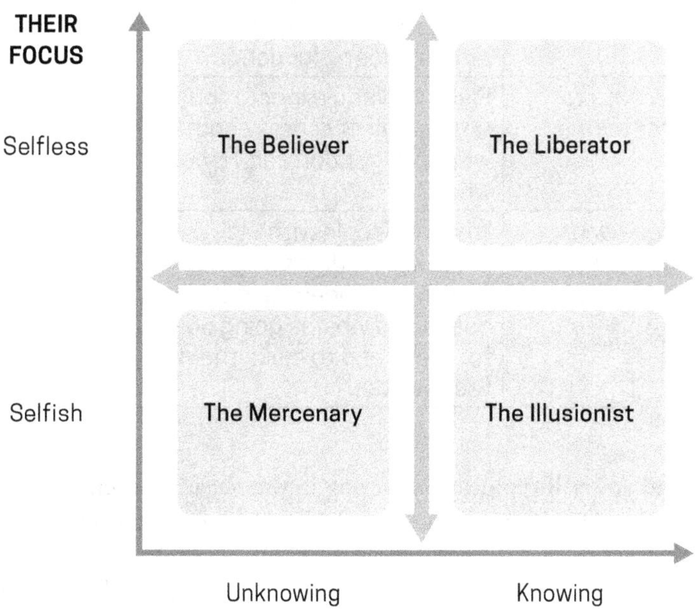

Figure 1.1: four types of boss

The Mercenary

With little to no awareness of their impact on others and caring primarily only about themselves, this boss operates in a bubble. They see themselves as all powerful and the smartest person in the room. It's all me, me, me! They have little interest in other people or in improving, because they believe they already have this leadership thing 'nailed'.

Their mantra: 'Don't get in the way of my success.'

Working for someone like this can be exceptionally challenging, because while you need to keep your head down, do the work and stay out of the firing line, you also need to not come across as weak. They see weakness as a character flaw and will use it against you. They won't welcome feedback, so be careful of any comments that appear to undermine their superiority, yet be strong and confident in the way you interact with them.

The Believer

This type of boss isn't a bad person; they just make an ineffective leader. With low self-awareness, they are largely oblivious of the negative impact they can have. In fact, they'll often think they are doing a great job leading, because they genuinely care about their team and try to put the team first.

Their mantra: 'Like me and be happy.'

Working for someone like this can be an opportunity for you to thrive once you find a way to work around their limitations. Seek to understand them and leverage ways to manage them. They are usually open to feedback, so you can talk to them about how you might better work together.

The Illusionist

This boss has a high awareness of their impact on others, and cares primarily about themselves. In many respects, they are worse than the mercenary, because they know the impact they are having, but either don't care or just can't find a way to change how they lead. They are good at managing up and can charm the pants off you, although when things go wrong you could find yourself under the bus.

Their mantra: 'Make me look good.'

The more you make them look good, the more they will want you around. This can be good for your development and there can be opportunities. But remember, they don't care that they don't care, so you will be expendable and have a use-by date. Like the mercenary, they won't welcome feedback, so be careful of any comments that might appear to undermine their superiority. Instead, ask questions about how you might better support them, while taking care of your own needs too.

The Liberator

With a deep awareness of their impact on others and a very caring attitude, the liberator always puts the team first. This is the ultimate good boss, and luckily there are many of them. This doesn't mean they are perfect every single day, because that's an unrealistic expectation. But they do care and they have self-awareness.

Consequently, when they stuff up and make a mistake, they own it. They will support you and your career aspirations. They won't just be nice and say what you want to hear. Instead, because they care, they will challenge you to do better and give you constructive, healthy feedback.

Their mantra: 'Let's work together productively.'

Working for someone like this is your opportunity to be your best. They are open to feedback and conversations, and you will learn much from them.

Which style do you think your boss exhibits?

Let's find out using the following three steps.

Step 1: Get curious

The first step is to critically examine your perspective of your boss's level of awareness of their impact on others, and whether or not it's intentional, using the following questions.

Awareness of impact (unknowing vs knowing)

Ask yourself, do you feel and think:

- their behaviour is deliberate and intentional?
- they are aware of the impact they have on you and other team members?

If you have answered 'yes' to those two questions, then it is likely your boss is aware of what they are doing. Their behaviour is carried out *knowingly*. If your answer is 'no', it is most likely carried out *unknowingly*.

Now think about their focus and whether they are putting themselves first, or considering the needs of others, using the following questions.

Their focus (selfish versus selfless)

Ask yourself, do you feel and think:

- their actions are primarily about them and their needs?
- they don't care about you and your needs?
- they ignore the challenges and workload you face?
- they show little interest in you as a person?
- they drive things too hard, disregarding the consequences for their team?

If you have answered 'yes' to those questions, then it is likely that your boss is taking a *selfish* approach to leadership, putting their own needs first. If your answer is 'no', they are *selfless*.

Find the points of intersection in figure 1.3 to determine what type of boss you have: mercenary, believer, illusionist or liberator.

Step 2: Source other opinions

It's important not to overplay instances of challenging behaviour. It can be easy to judge someone too harshly and to cast them into the 'bad boss' category based on a few instances when they haven't been at their best.

Alan Benson, Professor of Work and Organizations at the Carlson School of Management at the University of Minnesota, cautions against judging people too harshly based on a few memorable instances. 'People also tend to overweight first impressions and last impressions, compared to events that happened in the middle. These are called the primacy and recency effects.'

It can be helpful to get the perspective of a trusted colleague to challenge your views.

TIME OUT

- Are you being too harsh?
- Is your boss's current behaviour out of character?

In reflecting, look for consistency and be consistently fair.

Step 3: Check for mitigating factors

If their behaviour has changed in recent times, this step will help, because it's about understanding what may be driving their behaviour. To do this you must first be open and compassionate.

Dr Brené Brown, in her book *Dare to Lead*, writes about how you can change how you approach issues and people by assuming they are doing their best. 'The assumption of positive intent,' she suggests, 'is only sustainable when people ask themselves this question: What boundaries need to be in place for me to be in my integrity and generous with my assumptions about the intentions, words, and actions of others?'

Setting boundaries in this context is about making clear what's okay and what's not okay, and why.

Starting from the assumption that your boss is doing their best, what do you think is driving how they think and behave?

TIME OUT

- Are they under too much pressure from their boss?
- Is their workload unsustainable?
- Are their peers challenging to work with?
- Are there not enough resources in the team?

- Are they set up for success in the role, with the right team, the right resources, the right skill levels?
- Are they relatively new to the role and still settling in?
- What's happening in their personal life? Are they facing challenges on the home front?
- Has there been a recent change in their behaviour, and if so, what could be triggering that for them?

In answering these questions, you may find that one of the best things you can do to help the situation is to empathise with your boss and seek ways to support them.

Bosses are human too, and the environment may not be bringing out their best.

Pre-match check

In looking at all the data and insights you've collected, how much of the situation you confront at work is about you stepping up and changing, and how much sits with your boss?

You may still reach the conclusion that your boss is hard work or ineffective. Or perhaps your analysis has softened your perspective and you are willing to show them more compassion and understanding, and therefore to alter your behaviour first.

Whatever position you land on, it's not time to throw in the towel just yet! Reflecting on my career, some of the toughest jobs and hardest people to work for turned out to be pivotal and vital experiences in my career. While they may not have been nice to work with, the experience I gained often made it worthwhile in the long run.

So before you throw down this book and yell, 'Well, that's just confirmed my suspicions. My boss is a jerk!' consider the long-term benefits you can gain from the role. Reflect on what you are learning, the skills you are acquiring, the contacts you are making and whether it is setting you up for your next role, which will be bigger and better. Can you stick it out a bit longer with some help?

Of course, your health comes first, and you must ensure you are not suffering from bullying or interactions that are undermining your wellbeing. But as you'll see in the next chapter, there are strategies within your control that will help.

You can't change your boss, but you can influence their behaviour and how they treat you by taking the right strategic approach.

On the field

It would be great to fill this book only with happy stories, but sadly that wouldn't reflect the reality of our working world.

Take Kirsty, for example. She found herself in a very challenging workplace with a boss who made her life hell by putting her down in front of colleagues and constantly and very publicly criticising her work. This experience eroded her self-confidence.

Finally she took steps to leave. However, she initially found getting back into the market hard. Why? Because she had stayed in that negative environment for too long, which had a residual impact on her self-esteem. Over time, with coaching support, she got back on track and happily found a better role.

It's critical to address issues with your boss sooner rather than later so this doesn't happen to you too.

2 STRATEGISE YOUR OPTIONS

In the 2011 movie *Horrible Bosses*, starring Jason Bateman and a raft of other Hollywood actors, three mates share a problem: they work for a boss who is making their life miserable. They feel trapped, because quitting their job doesn't feel like a viable option, so they come up with what they think is a cunning plan to rid themselves of their horrible boss.

Fuelled by alcohol, bad advice from a career criminal and a serious lack of judgement, they devise a complex and harebrained scheme that gets them into a whole heap of trouble. As their plan for revenge unravels, they dig themselves into a deeper and deeper hole.

While the story makes for an amusing way to spend an evening, it offers little in the way of good career management advice.

> Boss-revenge schemes as a career enhancement strategy never work.

Sure, you may not enjoy the work environment or like working for your boss, but there's nothing to be gained by plotting revenge, cooking up crazy schemes of one-upmanship or sticking pins in a boss voodoo doll every evening. Such plans will come back to bite you, big time, as they did in the movie.

No matter how good it feels thinking about it, retribution won't help your situation. In fact, it's likely that you will be the one to suffer. You may come out looking like the 'bad employee' with a poor performance record, tarnishing your reputation and damaging your career advancement prospects. Also, people talk—all the time—and you never know 'who knows who', so what may seem harmless at the time could come back to haunt you down the track.

This doesn't mean you roll over and take whatever comes your way. You need to plan, think long term and be strategic about how you manage working with your boss. This is what managing up is all about! You need to be deliberate about what you do and why. Pick your battles and your timing, and be conscious of the need to manage the risks associated with your choices.

This isn't a one-size-fits-all situation. You can't say, 'Here's the type of boss I have [*insert label X*], which means I need to take action in this way [*insert label Y*].' There is no magic formula, no dependable sequence of events. And there's no guarantee that your approach will work.

You need to think through what you're doing continuously, test and apply it, then make adjustments according to the outcome.

Stop whingeing, start advancing

It's easy to bitch and moan about work and how much you hate your boss. While getting those emotions out of your head and expressing them by talking them through with a trusted colleague can be helpful, if you do that over and over it becomes unproductive and wasted energy (not to mention annoying for everyone around you).

No more 'woe is me', 'this sucks', 'why me' or 'it's their fault'. Those negative emotions won't help you. No more feeling like you are stuck on the bench and can't get onto the field.

To get match fit, you may be thinking that the key is finding a way to get your boss to change the game. Wrong answer! You can't change someone else, no matter how hard you try.

Change is up to you.

This means putting yourself on the field and going for the goal every time to ultimately advance your career success, as shown in figure 2.1.

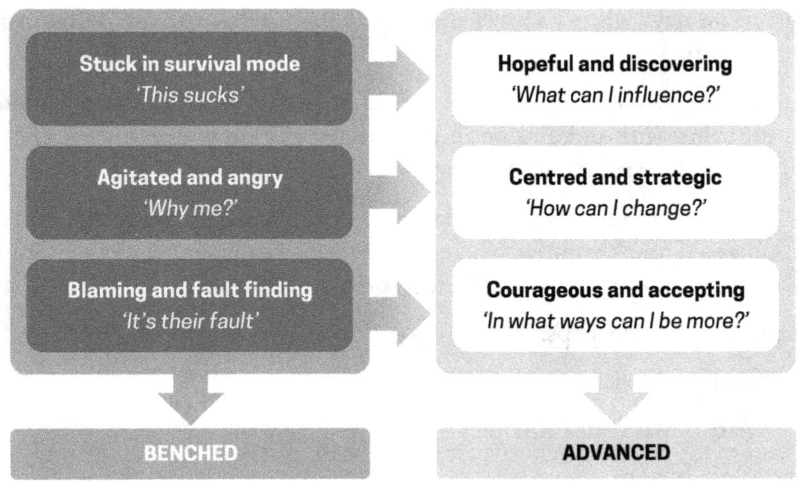

Figure 2.1: moving from benched to advanced

To do that you are going to develop a series of strategic options that are realistic, helpful and implementable. You'll focus your energy on what you can influence, rather than on things you can't change.

You will be mindful and strategic in the choices you make about what to do and when, always looking to enhance your reputation and uplift your performance outcomes. You will also challenge yourself to step up, so you can be your best every day, have courageous conversations, negotiate and take actions in ways that in the past you would have steered away from.

Along the way you will constantly check in to ensure you are strategically targeting your efforts and attention in the right direction, asking:

What can I influence?
How can I change or improve?

You go first

First, you need to document what it is you stand for, which comprises your vision and principles. This is your personal commitment to uphold your values and to act with integrity so your reputation flourishes.

Now you may be wondering, how does this help me deal with a bad boss? It helps because it centres you. It gives you direction and a reference point to return to on days when you feel challenged about what you are doing or not doing at work.

Think of your vision and principles as field markers that help ensure you don't cross the white line and end up in the wrong position where you sacrifice or compromise your values, and in time lose your integrity.

This doesn't mean you won't occasionally lapse, but when you reflect on your position you'll quickly notice where you've slipped or where you've developed, how to redress and refocus, and how to progress positively.

This process has two steps:

1. Frame your vision.
2. Write down your principles.

Let's explore each of them.

Step 1: Frame your vision

Just as organisations have a vision statement that anchors what they do, their purpose and their ambitions, so too should you.

> Your vision statement helps you remain focused on what really matters to you, and not be distracted by other people's agendas.

It helps to clarify the choices you make every day as you focus on the present, while looking ahead to the future. It gives meaning to your actions as you head towards your end goal. It helps you prioritise and push beyond your comfort zone, paving the way for a life of your design.

Here are some examples of vision statements:

- **Oprah Winfrey**: *To be a teacher. And to be known for inspiring my students to be more than they thought they could be.*
- **Maya Angelou:** *My mission in life is not merely to survive, but to thrive; and to do so with some passion, some compassion, some humour, and some style.*
- **Richard Branson:** *To have fun in my journey through life and learn from my mistakes.*

And mine

To create an abundant world rich with learning, opportunity and choice by living my life with courage, compassion and fairness.

TIME OUT

- What and who inspires you, and why?
- When have you been most motivated?
- What angers, frustrates or disappoints you?
- What are your two or three most important values?
- What do you want to be known and respected for at work?
- What difference do you want to make to the people you work with?
- When people talk about you, how would you like to be described?
- When have you been most proud of who you are as a person?

Answering these questions is designed to surface the elements in your working life that most matter to you.

A good vision statement will be future focused and directional, so it helps clarify the path you take. It will be specific and unambiguous, so it guides your decision making, as well being a little audacious, so it's aspirational and motivational.

Once you've settled on your vision—and no, it's not set in stone; you will continue to tweak it over the years—make it visible. I have my words written above my office desk, and accompanying those words are images of life that inspire me and keep me going when things get tough (or a little off kilter).

Step 2: Write down your principles

Underpinning your vision statement are the guiding principles and behaviours you strive to live by each day as you bring your vision to life. Think of them as your 'I statements'. My principles are as follows:

I will . . .

- live life as an adventure
- be fair and deliberate
- make each day matter
- put myself in the other person's shoes
- exercise, meditate and laugh daily
- bring music into my life
- live by the adage 'If you can't say something nice, don't say anything'
- step into the courageous conversations
- reflect and look for learning.

What principles and behaviours do you want to guide your decisions and actions as you strive to improve your current working environment?

I encourage you to push yourself—just a little. The statements you write down need to be true to who you are and to your values, but you may also need to include behaviours that are a little bolder and braver than what you would normally do. Challenge yourself: will these behaviours help or hinder your desired progress?

Check your position

I remember a time during my corporate career when I was faced with the stark knowledge that a colleague of mine had a negative view of me.

It all stemmed from the fact that I asked questions—lots of them. They thought my questioning was because I wanted to find fault with their work, when the truth was quite the reverse. I looked at how they approached problems and found it was very different from my own thought processes. I was curious, I wanted to know, understand and learn from them.

It was sobering for me to discover the damage that can arise when the intent of your behaviour is misconstrued. Thankfully, after a courageous conversation we discovered the gap in our mutual understanding and discussed our different perspectives, and this changed the nature of our working relationship.

How you want to be seen and how you are seen can often be quite different.

You can't possibly influence how people see you if you don't first know how you are seen.

This starts with having in place regular avenues of reliable feedback—and that includes feedback from the person you report to (yes, your bad boss—*eek!*). Also seek feedback proactively from people who will challenge you, while offering it from a place of good intent.

You need to understand in what areas you perhaps aren't meeting your boss's expectations. You also need to be aware of your reputation among other key stakeholders and colleagues.

You may find the two balance each other out. For example, if your boss thinks poorly of your work performance but you have other senior stakeholders who advocate for you, that can place you in a stronger negotiating position with your boss.

It can help to have a friend, colleague or professional mentor who will challenge your assumptions and perspectives. Use the information you glean from these conversations to identify where you need to change your game plan or raise your match fitness. You may need to change how you approach problems, broaden your expertise, strengthen your skills at influencing and relationship building, develop your resilience skills, and acquire or deepen specific capabilities and competencies.

Take a moment to consider who in your network is a good person to seek feedback from.

Once you've identified the gaps, it's up to you to find ways to close them. This may be through coaching, mentoring, formal training, on-the-job experience or learning from people around you who are good at what they do. Don't always expect your organisation to fund your learning and development. It's your responsibility too.

Invest in the boss bank

If you want your relationship with your boss to improve, you can't sit back and wait for *them* to improve it. Sure, relationships are a two-way street, so they need to turn up to the game, but proactivity pays off.

Look for opportunities to build connection, add value and take full accountability for making the relationship progress positively. Think of this as the boss-relationship dividend.

The more you invest strategically and wisely, the more it will pay off.

However, if the stocks never rise then you likely need to change your investment strategy and go somewhere else. But like all investment strategies, sometimes it pays to wait it out for a while.

I've always found the more I helped my boss look good and be successful in their role, the easier it made my working relationship. The pay-off for me: more interesting work, bigger promotions and more pay, and even more importantly, a working environment where I felt valued, supported and respected.

Michael Watkins, in his book *The First 90 Days*, outlines what you need to do to make your relationship with your boss work:

1. Take 100 per cent responsibility for making the relationship work.
2. Clarify mutual expectations early and often.
3. Negotiate timelines for the work you are doing.
4. Aim for early wins in areas important to your boss.
5. Pursue good feedback from those whose opinions your boss respects.

While his book focuses on what you need to do when you start a new job, this advice is worth following throughout your working career. It's crucial to know what your boss values and how they like to work. Once you have those two vital pieces of information you can soon work out how you can make their life easier and add value to their work. As part of this, seek to understand what drives and motivates their career choices, and also what worries them.

For example:

- Your boss may value control and always want to know what's going on. This means you should keep them informed and ensure there are no surprises!
- Your boss may hate detail and prefer to focus on the big picture. If that's the case, know when to involve them and when not to. Get them involved in the concept setting then check that you're empowered to go full steam ahead.

- Your boss may have a really tough boss and be worried about how that relationship is maintained. If they face pressure from above, be understanding and find out what you can do to help them. (That's why reading this book from start to finish is so crucial, because it will help you gain insights into what is likely happening for them.)

Customise your approach to fit their needs, rather than expecting them to do that for you.

If you are struggling with this part because you feel you have no idea what their expectations of you are, or their expectations keep changing, then I'd encourage you to do two things:

1. **Ask them**. Be direct and have a conversation with them about what they need from you. The conversation simply starts with 'Meeting your expectations is important for me. What else do you need from me?'
2. **Ask someone else**. If the conversation with your boss feels too hard, or perhaps you've tried it and not got anywhere, then find someone who knows them well (and whom you trust) and seek their advice and counsel.

It's impossible to meet expectations if you don't know what they are.

Know your currency

While it's critical to strive to meet your boss's needs, you need to know your needs and strive to have them met too.

Abraham Maslow first introduced his hierarchy of needs theory in 1943. He proposed that people are motivated to fulfil basic needs before moving on to other, more advanced needs. At the bottom of the hierarchy are the basic needs of food, water (physiological needs) and safety, followed by the psychological needs of belonging, relationships and self-esteem, while at the top of the hierarchy is self-actualisation, or the fulfilment of an individual's potential.

Maslow believed we have an inborn desire to reach for that final stage, to become all we can be, but we cannot do so before our more basic physiological and psychological needs are met. This theoretical framework can be usefully applied to the work environment, as illustrated in figure 2.2 (overleaf).

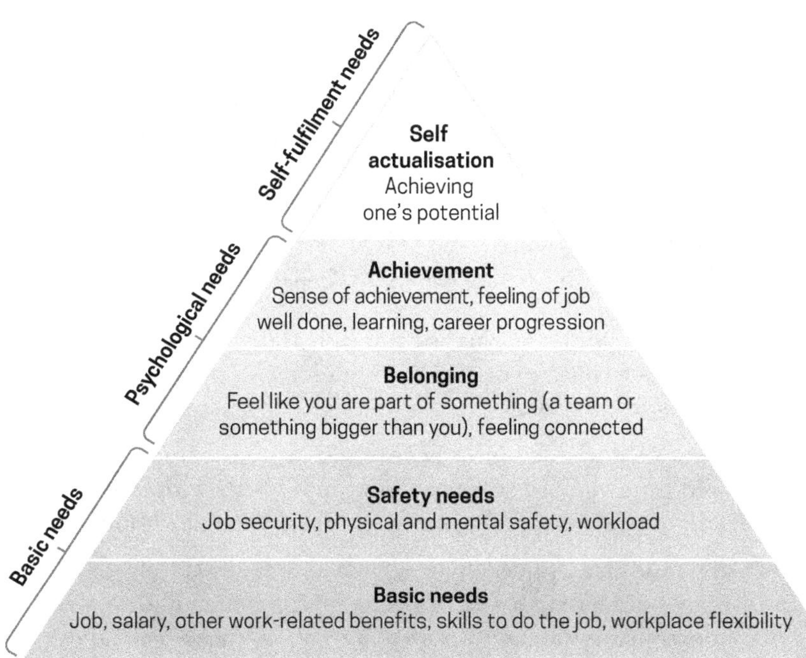

Figure 2.2: Maslow's hierarchy of needs, adapted for a workplace context

Unless you were born into or inherited money or have achieved financial independence through your own efforts, you will need an income to maintain a roof over your head and put food on the table. For some this means they'll take *any* job just to pay the bills. Many people also need a job that has a degree of flexibility so they can look after their family and dependants. Next, security needs must be satisfied. People want to work in a physically and psychologically safe environment. We hear a lot today about the importance of psychological safety and there's no doubt it's foundational to a good workplace culture. An unsafe workplace or toxic work culture will produce mental and physical distress.

Once these basic needs are met, the focus shifts to belonging and achievement. For most of us, a sense of belonging will take precedence. We are tribal creatures who place a high value on social connection. Even for today's 'liquid workforce' who have become accustomed to short-term contracts and uncertainty, we want to connect and be part of something. Achievement, on the other hand, is about feeling valued and recognised for the work we do.

Those seeking self-actualisation have generally reached an advanced stage in their career, where they only want to work in an environment where they can offer the most, be their best and achieve their full potential. Nothing less will satisfy them.

> Where you currently see yourself in the hierarchy and the emphasis you place on the five currencies will depend on your life circumstances.

Use table 2.1 to help you quickly assess what's important to you.

Table 2.1: your work value gap

	LEVEL OF DERIVED VALUE	
THE CURRENCY	**ARE THESE NEEDS BEING MET?** **YES/NO**	**WHICH NEEDS AREN'T BEING MET, AND WHY?**
Basic needs: Job, salary, other work-related benefits, skills to do the job, workplace flexibility		
Safety needs: Job security, physical and mental security, workload		
Belonging: Feel like you are part of a team, connected to something bigger than you		
Achievement: Sense of professional achievement, feeling of job well done, new learning, career progression		
Self-actualisation: Satisfaction of achieving your full potential at work		

Increasing the value

While the value you derive from your work is likely to change over time, ideally you want to be able to increase the value you get from your current job.

TIME OUT

- What would need to happen for more of your needs to be met?
- What actions can you take to enable more of your needs to be met?
- What actions would your boss need to take to enable more of your needs to be met?
- Could those needs be met in other ways to make staying in this job more palatable?

You need to focus on what you can control and influence, so some of this may be a future topic for discussion with your boss (the next chapter will help with this).

Pick your power play

One practice I often have my coaching clients do is called the premeditation of evils. It's a practice from the Stoic School of Philosophy, which harks back to ancient times. Philosophers such as Marcus Aurelius, Aristotle and Seneca used this technique.

The practice is designed to get you thinking about what could go horribly wrong in a tricky conversation (or situation). That way, if the issue arises you are prepared for it and better able to respond swiftly and positively. Most importantly, it encourages you to recognise that even if that worst-case scenario were to eventuate the action is still worth taking.

For example:

- What's the worst thing that could happen if you ask for a pay rise? Your boss says no, in which case you know where you stand and can now make a decision about what to do next.

- What's the worst thing that could happen if you talk to your boss about the impact work is having on you? They don't change or their behaviour gets worse, in which case you know it is definitely time to move on.

One of my clients was worried about talking to her boss about their working relationship. She thought he didn't like her work. I asked her, 'What's the worst thing that could happen if you have the conversation?' Her response: 'He might not renew my contract.' To which I replied, 'And how bad would that be if you hate your job?' She realised she didn't have that much to lose, so she had the conversation. It turned out he thought she was doing a fabulous job!

Reflecting on the possible outcomes often helps us realise that it's worth taking a risk and making the ask.

> If you don't put it out there it won't happen. If you do, you might be delightfully surprised by what you receive in return.

There will be a time to disagree and a time to remain silent. There will be times to voice your concerns one-on-one or more publicly. Pick your times. Pick your battles. But above all be deliberate and prepared. The more prepared you are for the conversation, and the likely ups and downs, the better placed you'll be to put forward your case. (We'll explore how to action tricky conversations in the next chapter.)

Set boundaries to deal with pester power

It pays to set the ground rules up front on how you and your boss work together.

This was always really hard for me because I'm a perfectionist and a people pleaser, and I would never want to disappoint my boss. If they dropped work on my desk at the last minute, I'd grumble but I'd do it. If emails came in over the weekend, I would action them.

Over time I'd get resentful. And yet I'd never said at the start that this wasn't okay. I learned over the years to work out what I will and won't do, particularly as it relates to out-of-hours work. That meant getting comfortable with saying 'no' and talking through my expectations and needs before I agreed to work for someone.

If you constantly say 'yes' to things you don't want to do, you ultimately give up your autonomy and disempower yourself.

The acclaimed author Paulo Coelho said, 'When you say "yes" to others, make sure you are not saying "no" to yourself.'

That doesn't mean you say 'no' without careful thought. Rather, it is saying 'no' with consideration and compassion for others *and* yourself. There's no doubt it can feel hard to say no and is often easier to say yes.

Marketing experts refer to a child's 'pester power'. When a child keeps pestering their parents to buy them something, often the parent will give in to the demands because it's much easier than dealing with the fallout from a refusal. Adults can be the same. We say 'yes', often reluctantly, because it's easier than explaining why we cannot help someone on this occasion, because we don't want to hurt their feelings, or we are worried about the ramifications of saying no.

There will be times when a no is unavoidable. You may be drowning in work and feeling unappreciated as more and more work comes your way. You may be asked to do something that goes against your principles or values. You may be asked to travel interstate for work at a time that means you'll miss an important family event.

Saying no in all these instances is easier when you have established boundaries around what you will and won't do, how you will respond to requests for work outside standard working hours, how you communicate with each other and other key factors — *before* the request comes in.

When faced with this dilemma, ask yourself: what's the right thing to do for you, others involved and the organisation? If the best course of action is to say 'no', use these four steps to deliver the message effectively:

1. Check the real reason for saying no and make sure it is legitimate and you are not simply being obstructionist.
2. Stand by your conviction, backing yourself and your decision not to do something. This means you deliver the message with compassion

and resolve, and you demonstrate understanding of your boss's perspective.

3. Be clear and specific about your reason for saying no when you talk with your boss. A blunt refusal can be interpreted as rude and unhelpful. Instead, express your position positively and explicitly. For example, 'I wish I could be involved, but I already have the agreed list of projects I need to finalise this quarter, so unfortunately I don't have the capacity to take on more. Happy to talk through how I might re-prioritise.'
4. Be genuine in your response and make sure you are open to hearing your boss's point of view. They have the right to express disappointment or discontent. Listen to their concerns and ensure they know you are keen to find a way to help, but you need their help to come up with a solution that satisfies both your needs.

Of course, this is easier to do if you are an employee who delivers results and delivers well — another reason why you play a central role in dealing with your difficult boss!

Reshape your role

Your job description outlines your role's key tasks and responsibilities. However, if you need a job where you feel like you can use your full potential, then don't restrict yourself to this description (what's written on that document). Instead, take an expansive approach.

There will often be opportunities to expand your role to include, for example, work you find intellectually stimulating, or tasks that enable you to acquire new skills and are beneficial to your career development.

Take the initiative and seek out those opportunities. As well as making your work more interesting, you'll be delivering more value than expected, which is good for your career progression.

Another way to increase the returns is to create your own reward and feedback scheme. If you find you're not getting the feedback you want from your boss, then build in your own feedback mechanisms. Humans find making progress motivating, so break your work down into smaller, bite-size chunks so you can see more regular progress. Don't wait for your organisation's internal reward and recognition scheme to kick into action. Instead, reward yourself. When you've hit a goal, reached a target or achieved something you've been striving for, reward yourself for your efforts in a way that's meaningful for you.

Seek connections

In his book *Vital Friends: The people you can't afford to live without,* Tom Rath outlines research indicating that employees who have best friends at work are seven times more likely to be engaged in their jobs. Additionally, if they have at least three vital friends at work, they are 96 per cent more likely to be satisfied with their job.

So it's not just the relationship with your boss you should focus on.

Strive to create a diverse network, including people you can turn to for advice and support. You want people around—both inside and outside the organisation—who will support and advocate for you, as well as people who can provide sound counsel and insights.

It's not a good career strategy to rely solely on your boss to advocate for you, help you advance and develop, and sing your praises to others. Some bosses are awesome at developing their teams, ensuring they receive credit for their ideas and efforts and supporting their career advancement. Sadly, that's not always the case.

If your boss is insecure and lacks confidence in their role, it's unlikely they'll talk you up for fear that those compliments will somehow reflect poorly on them, making them look deficient or less powerful and successful.

A strong internal support network can help counterbalance the challenges of working for someone who is difficult. Often the people in your network who are more senior will see your good work and may tap you on the shoulder to go and work with them. They can also be a great source of advice and ideas about how to manage your current challenging work environment without damaging your career. A good support network will help you going into the next chapter, because it's time for action now.

A strong network is a power-charger for your career that never goes flat!

On the field

Sara had recently been promoted to a more senior role. She loved the job and really enjoyed working with her boss. Then he resigned.

The first six months with the new boss were hard — really hard. Their operating styles were totally different, and she felt she was being micro-managed. The new boss didn't respond to emails and wanted to be across all the details.

Sara did the 'should I stay or should I go' analysis, and decided to dig in for a while, as she liked her job and the organisation. She knew she needed to find a way to improve the relationship, so she adjusted her style to suit his.

When she did that, her boss started to shift his style to accommodate her needs. Over time — about six months — a new rhythm came into play. There was banter, mutual respect and a growing appreciation of each other's differences and the talent each brought to their respective roles. Eventually she came to enjoy working for her new boss as much as for his predecessor.

Time, patience and practice can be your friend.

3
ACT
WITH INTENT

Reshaping the relationship with your boss won't be the result of one idea, one attempt or a single act of initiative. It will be the product of a series of courageous conversations, actions, responses and reflections.

It's now time to start enacting the ideas and options we explored in the previous chapter. It can be easy to put this off, thinking, 'I'll wait for the perfect time'. There is no perfect time. There's just *now* or *later*, and the problem with later is it often never arrives.

You also run the risk that if you take too long to act the underlying issue becomes even harder to deal with. A small crack in a relationship can widen and deepen if left untreated for a long time. You are much better off treating and repairing small cracks early and swiftly.

In her book *Dare to Lead*, Dr Brené Brown refers to these conversations and actions as your 'arena moments'. These are the moments when you are called to show up, be brave and walk into the arena despite your fears.

This may mean talking to your boss about an impact their behaviour is having on you. It may mean speaking up in a meeting in front of more senior stakeholders. It may mean saying 'no' to more work and setting boundaries. It may mean facing up to one of your unproductive behaviours and challenging yourself to be more.

In all situations it will require you to drop any defensive or unhelpful behaviour that's holding you back, and all the while hold true to your vision and principles (outlined in the previous chapter).

With action comes reward, but also risk. You need to be ready to act and be mindful of the risks. As the British prime minister, statesman and novelist Benjamin Disraeli wrote, 'Action may not always bring happiness, but there is no happiness without action.'

With every action there is also a potential for reaction or overreaction, so it's imperative you always start this process by checking the lens through which you are viewing the situation.

Flip the boss lens

People watching is one of my favourite pastimes. On one such occasion, I was fascinated by a very loud conversation between two people at the café table next to mine.

The person was evidently infuriated by someone at work who had let them down. Their stream of vitriol was peppered with a heap of assumptions. Assumptions about why their colleague had done what they'd done, how they'd acted, their level of competence (or incompetence), their work ethic and much more.

Now, this critic may have had very valid reasons for their complaints, and venting to a trusted friend can be a useful way to work out the best way to respond. What would have been more useful, however, would have been for them to step back and examine their perspective and interpretation of events, and to challenge themselves on the lens through which they were viewing the situation.

The same goes for interactions with your boss. You have already categorised them as 'bad' or 'difficult', so you have a heightened sensitivity to everything they say or do.

> When your boss does something that displeases or upsets you it can be easy to make snap judgements.

You may think they've failed to do something because they're lazy or selfish, or that they are late for a meeting because they're disorganised, or that they don't appreciate the work you've done because they don't like it. But is this true?

In many such situations, your judgement can be way off the mark. It's time to start flipping the lens you use to view your boss and their actions. This starts with you metaphorically taking off your glasses and polishing or changing the lenses to ensure you're seeing the world as it really is.

Our brain wants to keep us safe, so it is always on the alert for 'red flags', warning signs of impending danger. This means it is also more attuned to the negative than the positive, and it can catastrophise really quickly.

Here are just three examples:

- Your boss doesn't invite you to a meeting—and you think, 'OMG, he hates me'.
- Your boss doesn't respond to an email regarding a critical report you've been working on for months—and you think, 'She thinks my work is useless'.
- Your boss praises a work colleague—and you think, 'They never say nice things about me. I reckon I'm about to get fired'.

We catastrophise like this when we are in 'fight or flight' mode, that emotionally charged state in which the brain's cognitive reasoning side isn't working optimally. In this state, you'll have reduced ability to reason and to solve complex problems, and you'll also be far more likely to see another person's actions as a threat.

This is not a great place to be, and not a good place from which to make a sound assessment of what's going on and how to respond.

It's imperative to notice when you've been triggered in this way, because when you are aware of it you can take steps to shift your state. This might involve removing yourself from the situation, finding quiet time for reflection or going for a walk—any action that enables you to slow your racing mind.

> The breath is crucial because it reactivates your brain's cognitive reasoning part.

When your boss does something that upsets you, get curious about what's driving your boss's behaviour. There's a difference between a boss who is a good person but in a stressful situation and not coping very well, and a boss who thrives on power and is a narcissist or a bully.

For example, if they are stressed because of work pressures, find out if there are ways you can help them with their workload. Challenging times always create opportunity, because the more you help them out, the more they will rely on you. This elevates your position in the relationship.

TIME OUT

- In what ways can you be more supportive of your boss?
- Do you know what your boss needs from you to help them be their best?
- If you were more understanding and compassionate about the challenges they face, what would you feel, think and do differently?
- If you adopt the perspective that they are doing their best, how does this change what you will say and do?

The more they need you, the more bargaining power you have when you negotiate.

A nudge in the right direction

Before you head into any tough conversation it's important to remember a basic rule of negotiation, which is that if you want to be successful don't ask for something the other person can't give you.

It's the same with relationships. If you want your boss to be a 'buddy-buddy' type and they aren't of that ilk, then your expectations are out of kilter. Similarly, if you want your boss to be methodical and reliable and they are fundamentally disorganised, you are setting yourself up for disappointment.

Your boss won't change their personality for you. However, there are ways to subtly nudge their behaviours in more desirable directions.

Try this:

1. Think of the behaviour of your boss that frustrates or annoys you.
2. Identify the actions or processes you could put in place to mitigate that behaviour.
3. Talk to your boss (or, in some cases, their EA) to see if your suggestion will work. Pitch it in a way that doesn't undermine their ego but makes them look and feel good and important.
4. Test how the new approach works, and tweak it if necessary.

If your boss always delegates tasks to you at the last minute, talk to their EA (if they have one) and find out if there's a way to get advance notice. If there's no EA involved, talk directly to your boss. Tell them how keen you are to help them and that the more notice you get of delegated tasks, the better you'll be able to do them. Sometimes this will feel hard and require you to step into your personal power.

Power is often seen as a negative, and that's because it is usually associated with the idea of exercising 'power over other people'. Think of the bullying boss, the so-called 'strongman' leader of a repressive dictatorship or the person at work who wields power as a weapon in their struggle to reach the top.

Ena Inesi, Associate Professor of Organisational Behaviour at London Business School, argues, 'Power is shifting, it's fleeting. It's relative and it's always about what matters in that moment—what is the value currency?'

Think of the traditional currencies of power: money, status, hierarchy and expertise. What is valued over time changes, so who has power and who doesn't changes over time too. Where this doesn't apply is to the power that resides within you. It's not fleeting, and its value is what you want it to be. You have the choice to step into your power or step away from it.

When you step into it you are willing to speak up even when it's uncomfortable, to have the tough conversations and to make decisions even if it means some people won't like you. When you step away from your power, you walk away from your right to have a voice, effectively giving it to someone else.

> Having a voice and using your internal power are essential for a healthy dynamic with your boss.

When you lose your voice and ability to speak up, the power imbalance in the relationship, based on your boss's positional authority, becomes even greater.

Once you know how and when to use your voice and back yourself, you'll start to see the balance of power within the organisational system improve. When power is more equally distributed it is easier to challenge assumptions, to act collaboratively and to make better-informed and considered decisions.

Madeleine Albright, the first female US Secretary of State, has observed, 'It took me quite a long time to develop a voice, and now that I have it, I am not going to be silent.'

Negotiate your position

All relationships involve give and take. In many situations, regardless of the topic, treating the conversation you are about to have with your boss as a negotiation can be a useful approach to take. It's the art of compromise and relationship building.

When you enter the arena, be ready to negotiate.

This doesn't mean you thump the table, throw a log of claims at them and go on strike until your demands are met. Rather, you recognise that the best outcomes are often negotiated outcomes, so there is much you can learn from looking at how the best have done it.

Harvard Law School named the late Nelson Mandela as one of the best negotiators in history. He was known for his patience, resolve, practical approach, ability to think strategically and to persevere. He knew when to yield and make concessions, but he wouldn't back down on what really mattered.

Jeff Weiss, Aram Donigian and Jonathan Hughes studied how US military officers resolve conflict and influence others in situations of extreme risk and uncertainty. The researchers found that the most skilled negotiators deployed five strategies:

1. Understand the big picture. Know the other person's agenda and point of view.
2. Uncover hidden agendas and collaborate with the other side. Propose multiple solutions and invite the other side to collaborate and share their ideas.
3. Get genuine buy-in. Use facts and principles of fairness to persuade and influence.
4. Build relationships based on trust rather than fear. Constantly seek incremental steps to move forward with trust.
5. Pay attention to process as well as desired outcomes. Don't react to the other side; instead, take steps to shape the negotiation process as well as the outcome.

The same principles apply to challenging conversations with your boss. You need to understand the bigger picture and what's going on for them. Check in on whether there are agendas you aren't yet aware of that might influence their decisions.

It's also crucial to enter the conversation having already identified multiple solutions to the issue you want to discuss with them.

With that knowledge to hand, be ready to compromise in order to shift and shape the options. You are far more likely to be successful if what you are asking for is fair and there is give and take and trust in the relationship.

Getting ready to step into the negotiating arena and engaging in a productive and constructive conversation with your boss has five key elements, though they are not necessarily sequential steps.

Let's look at each now.

1. Be open-minded and open-hearted

Negotiations often take unexpected turns, and it's very easy for the situation to escalate. You need to respond mindfully, rather than reactively. So don't negotiate or enter into difficult conversations when you are tired. If you find your mind is racing, focus on your breath and breathing deeply. This allows time for your nerves to settle and your heart rate to slow down, making it easier to reflect and respond calmly.

Be respectful, make sure they feel heard and back yourself. This isn't the time to get judgemental, argumentative or belligerent, or to throw your weight around. It's about strategically putting forward your opinion in a calm and unemotional way.

TIME OUT

- Are you bringing your best self to this conversation?
- Have you picked a good time of day to have the conversation?
- Are you approaching this conversation with a growth mindset?
- Are you ready to open your heart, and to listen and learn?
- Are you ready to take accountability for your role in this relationship?

2. Have clear options

Understand what you want from the negotiation, and don't be afraid to ask for it. It may be a case of 'don't ask—don't get'. So be deliberate about your needs and when to ask. Timing can be crucial, as a negotiation's starting position can anchor the rest of the conversation. Take the time to understand the options available and how your proposal could satisfy your boss's needs. Additionally, be clear on both your non-negotiables and what you are willing to give up.

TIME OUT

- Have you done your homework?
- Do you know your motivations and needs, and is your intent sound?
- Have you identified the potential options and your desired outcome?
- What are you willing to trade off and what matters most to you?
- What are your concerns, assumptions or preconceived ideas about your boss and their likely reaction to this conversation?
- What are the biggest hurdles that could prevent this conversation from being successful?
- What are the biggest opportunities for you in this conversation?
- How much do you care about this conversation (both the person and the outcome) and why?

3. Understand your boss's needs

Seek to understand your boss—their operating style, agenda and needs, and what they care about. The more you understand, the greater insights you'll have into what they are likely to support or reject.

TIME OUT

- What are their motivations and agenda?
- How have they responded to past requests?
- What's currently worrying them?
- What are their likely objections?
- What's their likely desired outcome?
- What's the best time of day to have this conversation with them?
- Do they have the authority and resources to give you what you want?
- How much are they likely to care? What are the implications/ consequences for them?

4. Conduct your pre-mortem

To help elevate a project's chance of success, author and scientist Gary Klein advocates conducting a *pre-mortem* (also known as prospective hindsight). This technique is used at the beginning of a project to surface potential reasons why it could fail. It's different from a risk analysis, where you seek to discover what risks may arise during a project by asking 'what could go wrong?' With this approach, potential risks are highlighted by assuming the worst-case scenario for the project has occurred, and asking 'what did go wrong?'

Klein writes, 'Unlike a typical critiquing session, in which project team members are asked what *might* go wrong, the premortem operates on the assumption that the "patient" has died, and so asks what *did* go wrong.'

In this exercise, every team member is asked to write down the reasons why the failure occurred, and those results are analysed. Klein has found that this approach not only helps teams identify potential problems early and sensitises people to the early-warning signs of issues as the project starts; it also helps stop people from becoming overinvested in a project and digging in too deep when problems arise.

I love this idea because it gets you thinking about what can go wrong. This isn't so you immediately stop and don't proceed; rather, it's so you go ahead with your eyes wide open and are ready for the potential risks and issues that could arise.

> In the context of the relationship with your boss you can use the same technique to ensure you are ready to act and respond if things don't go to plan.

For example, you may be planning to have a courageous conversation about your working relationship. As part of your pre-mortem process, you'll think through how the discussion may unfold, looking at the many options that could be taken at each stage. You'll also map out all possible outcomes, including, at one extreme, the conversation going completely pear-shaped, resulting in you feeling you should resign.

This isn't to scare you or to stop you from proceeding. It is to prepare you for all potential issues and outcomes — the good, the bad and the not-so-bad.

Let's run through the pre-mortem process now. Think about something you want to do — whether it's a frank conversation with your boss, or something else entirely.

TIME OUT

- List all the reasons why this conversation (or whatever it is you are planning on doing) might be derailed. Include ideas that even on the surface seem completely implausible.
- What is the likelihood that those negative issues will occur?
- If they do, what are the possible consequences and what will you do to manage or mitigate them?
- In light of those insights, how will you approach the conversation with your boss differently?

5. Have resolve and see it through

Depending on the nature of the conversation, its complexity and the emotion attached to it, be prepared for it to take time. It's better to progress slowly than to rush and get nowhere.

No matter where it comes from, when you feel more powerful you are more powerful, and you will likely get better outcomes in negotiations. Dutch researchers Alain Hong and Per van der Wijst of Tilburg University asked people to recall times when they had power over one or more people, while a control group were asked to write about how they spent their evenings.

The groups then entered into a series of negotiations. The results showed that women who were primed to feel powerful made much more aggressive first offers and negotiated better outcomes for themselves than the women in the control group did. Interestingly, men reached similar outcomes whether or not they were primed to feel powerful.

In certain situations it pays to seek permission to put forward your views. This isn't about being overly deferential; it's about opening the door to new ideas. For example, if your boss puts forward a proposal you disagree with, ask them if they are open to hearing a different perspective on the topic.

TIME OUT

- Are you ready to accept the consequences — even if they are to your disadvantage?
- Does this matter enough to you that it's worth the effort, energy and risk to invest in it?
- Are you ready to dig in, be courageous and have this conversation?

The first time you step into the arena for the conversation with your boss, you'll be nervous. That's natural. Don't let the fear hold you back. Countless times in my career it was stepping forward — first and early — that set me up for a successful relationship with my boss.

Aim for the 3 Cs

It's important at this point to talk about stress — and more specifically, how to deal with it when you're working in a stressful situation. When you are busy and stressed it can be easy to let prioritising your health fall by the wayside.

It's more important than ever to maintain mechanisms for self-care to help you manage stress.

Early in my career, I would regularly sacrifice my health for a meeting, a deadline or a work-related emergency. Over time, I realised I couldn't be effective, productive or at my best if I turned up tired, stressed or grumpy. I learned that prioritising my health needs was just as important as meeting a deadline.

Your diet, sleep patterns and exercise program all impact your cognitive performance and how you feel. Not getting enough sleep, for example, causes the same level of cognitive impairment as if you are drunk, and I can't imagine that turning up at work drunk is a good indicator that you are prepared for a productive working day!

It's about setting yourself up for success by maintaining a specific self-care plan, regular exercise routines and core rituals that nourish your body and soul, and doing whatever you need to do to be in the best physical, mental and spiritual shape.

In the late 1970s, Dr Suzanne Kobasa at the University of Chicago found that executives who handled stress well had a 'hardiness' that was underscored by three characteristics (what I call the 3 Cs)—commitment, control and challenge. These traits decreased their risk of developing stress-related health problems by 50 per cent.

Her study involved 200 executives from a US company, Bell Telephone, that was undergoing radical restructuring. She found that having these personality traits didn't mean the executives didn't experience stress, but they had a better ability to deal with it.

The 3 Cs can be summarised as follows:

- **Commitment.** This means having a clear purpose, feeling good about your life and being involved in activities that give you a sense of connection and meaning. If you think back to the vision exercise you did in the previous chapter, this is why having a vision statement is so powerful.
- **Control.** This is all about how much control you 'feel' you have. The greater your perceived control, the greater your ability to cope with stress. Part of this depends on your locus of control—is it internally or externally driven? People with an external locus believe they have little or no control over their life and what happens to them—it's 'all down to fate'. By contrast, when you have an internal locus of control you know you can't control external events or other people, but what you can control is your reaction. An internal locus best helps you manage stress.
- **Challenge.** Do you view change as a positive challenge and an opportunity to learn, grow and develop? You are more likely to experience stress if you associate change with danger or threat.

These three traits can be harnessed through your:

1. mindset and learning
2. energy and focus
3. decisions and actions.

Let's look at these factors now.

1. Understand your mindset

When you approach challenges with a growth mindset you'll focus on the learnings. Rather than throwing your hands up in despair, thinking 'I'm a failure', you'll view mistakes as an opportunity to experiment, learn and grow. You'll view frustrations with your boss as an opportunity to explore a different side of yourself and to show compassion and empathy.

We learn things from everyone we work with, whether they are good or bad or somewhere in between. For example, working with a bad boss can shape your leadership style, because the experience can provide you with lessons on how *not* to lead.

This search for learning expands your understanding of self and of others.

TIME OUT

- Do you have a fixed or growth mindset?
- What are you learning today about yourself and your boss?
- What are you learning about what triggers different reactions in you?
- Are you open to change, welcoming the challenge of adapting and learning?

2. Focus your energy

In his bestseller *The 7 Habits of Highly Effective People* (still one of the most valuable self-development books ever written), Stephen Covey explains how too often we waste our energy on things we are concerned about but have zero, zip ability to change or influence, and that we are far better to focus our energy on the things we can influence.

> You can't control your boss, just as you can't control every curveball that life throws at you. What you can control is the meaning you put on that curveball and how you respond to it.

Recognising and accepting the difference is a crucial step towards acting productively and effectively. When dealing with your workplace challenges you will constantly check in on this.

When your energy is positively charged you are grateful for what you have. You are generous to others, and focus on sharing and supporting those around you.

Research from the Greater Good Science Center indicates that one of the keys to wellbeing is practising gratitude. Gratitude has been found to increase happiness levels and positive emotions, improve relationships and increase our resilience. People who are grateful for what they have are happier and more content with their lives.

TIME OUT

- Is your locus of control internally or externally focused?
- Are you focusing your attention on things you can control or influence?
- What unproductive work habits are impeding your progress and depleting your energy?
- Are you grateful for what you have or forever frustrated about what you don't have?
- Do you regularly play the comparison game, comparing yourself and your circumstances with those of others?

3. Decide to act mindfully

A key part of applying a growth mindset and focusing your energy is being mindful, rather than mindless. This ensures you are responding, rather than just reacting.

Mindfulness expert Jon Kabat-Zinn defines mindfulness as 'paying attention in a particular way: on purpose, in the present moment, and nonjudgmentally'.

When you are mindful you focus on the present, rather than rehashing the past or dwelling on the future.

Mindfulness works because it helps you to become aware of how you are feeling and then to step back from those feelings to work through how to respond, rather than getting caught up in the emotion and merely reacting.

With every interaction there is a decision. With every decision there is a choice — to be mindless or mindful.

When you are 'mindless' you don't notice that you have been triggered — your feelings and emotions activated — so an instantaneous behavioural reaction occurs, with little thought as to the impact it will have.

When you are mindful, the same comment or action will still trigger feelings and emotions, but you will be aware that you've been triggered and notice your immediate impulse. Rather than reacting, you will reflect on the underlying feelings and only then respond. This is you stopping, breathing, noticing, reflecting and responding.

While being mindful and meditating are different, they are strongly connected. I find the meditation practice that helps to quieten my mind also helps me be more mindful. It enables me to connect and notice and be fully aware of my feelings, to slow the chatter in my brain and any overthinking, and only then to respond.

TIME OUT

- Do you typically react mindfully or mindlessly?
- Do you notice what triggers your reactions?
- In stressful situations, do you breathe deeply, pause and reflect before you respond?
- Are you using regular practices like meditation to prepare yourself for stressful situations and enable good decision making?

These practices will not only help you be more centred and resilient; they will also lay the groundwork for you to be more open-minded in your interpretation of your boss.

Break the drama binge

Progress is not linear. You'll have days when you'll experience lots of forward momentum, and days when it feels like you are going backwards. On the days when your boss is driving you nuts and your relationship renovation plan feels like it is crumbling around you, it can be easy to turn to teammates and colleagues and complain about how bad your boss is.

It's comforting to vent your frustration and share your pain with a colleague. You feel relieved and validated when they confirm your assessment of your boss's character. It feels good to list your boss's faults, and to imagine scenarios in which you win and come out on top.

Gossiping, which is part of our evolutionary psychology, makes us feel good. Robin Dunbar, author of *Grooming, Gossip and the Evolution of Language*, explains that it's a form of social behaviour that helps large groups bond. We feel connected with someone when we gossip, and we like being part of the in-group when someone shares a secret with us.

> It's as easy to get caught up in workplace dramas as it is to get hooked on TV shows like *Survivor, The Bachelor* and *Married at First Sight.*

We sit back in front of the TV and watch the drama unfold. We assess the contestants from all angles. Laugh or cringe over their misfortune, mock what they do and say and how they look. We judge, ridicule and compare. We cheer for the underdog and hope the TV show villain (because there's always one) is undone. We watch the appointed villain plot and scheme, eagerly waiting for them to get knocked off their perch. All in the name of light-hearted entertainment.

At work, people gossip and size up their co-workers, revel in the misfortune of those they don't like, spread rumours and innuendo, and play politics.

Be honest and check yourself by circling which of the following apply to you. Do you:

- enjoy the office intrigue? [never, sometimes, always]
- create drama? [never, sometimes, always]
- find yourself in the middle of the workplace crisis? [never, sometimes, always]
- gossip about your colleagues and/or boss? [never, sometimes, always]

- have to be 'in the know'? [never, sometimes, always]
- pass on secrets confidentially shared with you? [never, sometimes, always]
- make a big deal of small things? [never, sometimes, always]
- overreact? [never, sometimes, always]

If you find yourself more often than not in the 'sometimes' or 'always' category, you'll need to consider how this behaviour is helping or hindering your reputation and the relationship with your boss.

The 16th-century English bishop, moral philosopher and satirist Joseph Hall wrote, 'A reputation once broken may possibly be repaired, but the world will always keep their eyes on the spot where the crack was.'

> Being labelled the office gossip won't enhance your career.

You can overshare at work, later wishing you'd kept your own counsel, particularly if the comments about your boss get back to your boss or other influential stakeholders.

Gossiping isn't productive behaviour. It's not getting on the field, being in control, investing in the boss-bank and going for goal. In the words of Elsa from the hit children's movie *Frozen*, there will be times when you just need to 'let it go'.

So when you've had a bad day, before you seek to offload and gossip check your intent in doing so:

1. Are you sharing as a way of offloading your hurt on someone else, or because you want to bring someone else down to your level?
2. Is it just unproductive gossip that's all about making your boss 'the enemy' and making you feel better?
3. Have you considered that your so-called trusted colleague might not do you any favours with that piece of information you have shared?

Sharing how you feel is healthy as long as it is constructive, you've selected wisely who you will share with, and the discussion is future focused rather than filled with recriminations and retribution.

Many years ago I worked with a person who said to me, 'Michelle, you can get to a certain level in your career by being good at what you do. But if you want to go any further, you need to know how to play the political game.'

The idea that you have to play politics and be Machiavellian to be successful in the corporate world always troubled me. In an interconnected world where your reputation sticks to you like glue, adopting such a philosophy can have long-term negative consequences.

You need to be fully aware of relationships in organisations and be part of a strong and vibrant network of people who support you.

> Plotting revenge, playing politics and seeking to undermine your boss will never help; acting with integrity, making wise choices and backing yourself will.

On the field

It's imperative that you tailor your message and approach to the circumstances and your boss. Different tactics will work at different times.

Kate's new boss had the horrible habit of standing at his desk and summoning her by yelling across the room. She found it demeaning. So she began ignoring him when he yelled, forcing him to come to her. He'd huff and puff when he got to her desk: 'Didn't you hear me?' She'd smile sweetly and calmly respond, 'No I didn't. How can I help you?' Eventually he learned to stop yelling, because it didn't help him get what he needed.

Toni struggled with her boss's behaviour because he was openly rude and difficult to deal with. One day he barged into her office announcing angrily, 'I have a complaint to make'. She responded with a laugh. 'I've had lots of those today, and I've no more room for complaints handling.' She proceeded to ask him how he was, and he happily sat down and calmly talked about his day.

In each case the unexpected approach disarmed a rude boss, persuading him to change his behaviour to get what he wanted. Humour too can be a very powerful instrument of influence!

4
REFLECT
ON PROGRESS

The classic children's tale *The Story of Ferdinand* by Munro Leaf, first published in 1936, is so popular that it has never been out of print. Ferdinand isn't your typical bull. All the other bulls around him dream of being chosen to compete in the bullfight in Madrid, but Ferdinand prefers to roam free and smell the flowers in the field.

One day Ferdinand is stung by a bumblebee, which sets him running wildly across the field, stamping and snorting. As fate would have it, at that moment he is spotted by some men whose job it is to select a bull for the upcoming running of the bulls in the capital. Mistaking him for a mad and aggressive bull, he is renamed 'Ferdinand the Fierce' and taken to Madrid.

When the bullfight begins, though, Ferdinand shows no interest in fighting the matador; he is attracted by the flowers adorning the women spectators' hair. So he lies in the middle of the ring to enjoy them.

Everyone is mad at him — the banderilleros, the picadores and the matador — but Ferdinand is happy. Eventually he is taken back to his pasture and his flowers to live out a peaceful and contented life.

> If meeting the expectations of your boss means you have to change who you are and be something different you have to wonder, is it worth it?

Trying to be something you are not is stressful. So it's important to reflect on the progress you've made in improving the relationship with your boss, as well as on the impact it's having on you.

Because you will constantly face moral and ethical choices, it is essential to be in an environment that brings out your best, where you feel comfortable and safe to be you.

Reflect, learn and grow

You hear the phrase 'fail fast' in organisations and tech companies a lot these days. In fact, it's often misused, primarily because most organisations who say they value failure actually don't. The philosophy that underpins it, however, is valuable.

It's based on a belief that when you want to implement a new idea, product, process or project, you should undertake extensive testing and incremental development to determine whether it works. It's about cutting your losses — quickly — so when the testing reveals that something isn't working, you pivot and try something else.

Managing Partner of Techstars and serial entrepreneur David Brown explains: 'Fail fast isn't about the big issues, it's about the little ones. It's an approach to running a company or developing a product that embraces lots of little experiments with the idea that some will work and grow and others will fail and die.'

It's the same for you. Some of your strategies and actions will go well, others not so well. It's important to constantly reflect and determine what's working and what's not, so you can adjust your strategy and approach quickly.

Consider in what ways you are making progress and in what ways you aren't. Which of your selected strategies are working well, and which ones don't appear to be having a positive impact?

Healthy progress means reflecting, not ruminating.

When we ruminate it's unproductive, because our thinking process doesn't reach a conclusion. We run the scenario in our head again and again, trying to rewrite how the event unfolded. It's like a broken record that keeps spinning and there's no off switch. This can lead to a range of negative outcomes — depression, anxiety, overeating or drinking, for example.

Reflecting, on the other hand, means learning. Researchers Giada Di Stefano, Francesca Gino, Gary Pisano and Bradley Staats found performance differed when a person's learning is coupled with reflection—'thinking after completing tasks is no idle pursuit: it can powerfully enhance the learning process, and it does so more than the accumulation of additional experience on the same task.'

So if you've had a conversation with your boss that went off the rails, or a negotiation where you didn't get what you wanted, reflect on why it unfolded as it did and what you could do differently next time.

TIME OUT

- How prepared were you for the conversation?
- Did you hold back from saying what you wanted to say? If so, why?
- What do you think was going on for your boss at the time?
- What was the outcome? Are you happy with the outcome?
- How did you feel at the start of the interaction (for example, busy, relaxed, distracted or something else)?
- Were you relaxed during the conversation (or not), and how did that affect the outcome?
- How did you feel by the end of the conversation?

Given all those insights, the next question to ponder is what will you do differently next time?

A progress stocktake

Just as retail stores conduct regular stocktakes, you'll want to undertake a more detailed assessment to check that the progress you are making is sufficient. If it isn't, the dilemma around 'should you stay or go' may become clearer.

In figure 2.2 (on page 28) you assessed your current level of workplace satisfaction against five currencies—basic, safety, belonging, achievement and self-actualisation. You determined which of those were or were not currently being met at work, and identified strategies to potentially enable more of them to be met. That is, to get more value from your current job.

Once again, look at each of those currencies and ask yourself which of them are being met. After that, consider whether you have plateaued, or are going backwards and fulfilling less of them, or whether more of those needs are now being met.

Hopefully you've discovered there's been great progress and you feel like the relationship dynamic has shifted and genuine improvement has been made. That's awesome! The hard work has paid off.

Keeping relationships thriving always takes effort.

This is not the time to sit back and cruise. Great relationships are the result of constant care and attention. You've made progress — don't let it slide. Look at what's worked and keep that going. Check to see if there are other strategies you now need to apply.

If you aren't happy with your progress, then the next step is to look at whether it's possible for your desired needs to be met by your boss and the work environment. Are your expectations realistic, and how hard are you prepared to work to realise those expectations?

TIME OUT

- Are your expectations realistic and is it possible for further change?
- Is your boss capable of helping to secure your desired needs?
- What more can you do to have those needs met?
- Is the risk and effort involved in securing the change worth it?

You may decide to abandon some strategies, but be cautious of giving in too quickly. Sometimes it can take a while for benefits to flow through. There's likely to be new strategies you need to apply, and others you need to tweak and continue.

If after completing this exercise you realise you have key unmet needs and the situation isn't likely to improve, then you need to assess your position and whether it's time to cash out.

Know when to cash out

Different people value different things and have different needs in relationships. Knowing the currencies that most matter to you and the gap that still exists enables you to be clear on what's a 'nice to have' and what's 'imperative' in the relationship with your boss.

For example, I never needed to be friends with my boss, but I did need to respect them and see them as someone I could learn from. Curiously, the best bosses did—over time—become friends. If I wasn't learning in my job (and from my boss) I'd get bored and leave.

In my corporate career, I worked hard to make my way up the corporate food chain to senior levels. I put success down to hard work, and my ability to get things done and build good relationships. Then I moved to a new organisation, where success eluded me. No matter how hard I worked, or how good my team was, I couldn't satisfy my boss's expectations.

I thought the currencies at risk for me were achievement and self-actualisation. But it was more than that. I just couldn't see it. I was risking my mental health as a result of the hours I was working. My husband saw it and one weekend he said, 'You have to get out. That place is killing you. I've never seen you second guess yourself so much. It's destroying your self-confidence.'

He was right. I had to face the fact that no matter what strategy I deployed, the situation would not change. Come Monday morning I told my boss I was going.

Deep down I knew it wasn't working and my needs weren't being met. I admired my boss's intellect (and he was a nice person), but I didn't enjoy his working style. He delayed making decisions and constantly changed his mind, which had huge impacts on my and the team's workload. I walked away with no job to go to because I couldn't achieve results or be who I needed to be. It was one of the hardest things I've ever done. In the long run it turned out to be one of my best decisions.

In his book *The Art of Stillness*, travel writer Pico Iyer, whose writing highlights the importance of having space and quiet time, writes about how so much of our lives takes place inside our heads—memory, imagination, interpretation or speculation—so if you want to change your life, he argues, it starts by changing your mind.

This is so true. You can't change how your boss thinks and feels. In some situations—not always—you can influence how they behave towards you by changing their opinion of you.

If you are working for a boss in a workplace where the pressure is relentless, the environment is toxic and there is no end in sight, then it's time to assess the impact it's having on your wellbeing.

Pressure can become unhealthy when you feel like you:

- have no control or autonomy
- are making little or no progress, or are going backwards
- have so much to do it feels overwhelming—constantly
- are ruminating about the same issues—again and again
- feel your confidence is shattered
- feel isolated and lack support in the work environment.

These are also the first signs that you could be headed towards burnout.

> When you get to the point that your work is making you so unhappy that it's affecting your wellbeing, you need to consider 'voting yourself off the field'.

Watch for fallout

A number of years ago I was working with a client who faced constant pressure at work. The leadership team she was a part of had a toxic culture, and it was commonplace for people to be publicly humiliated and yelled at in meetings by the CEO.

My client's behaviour and style were at the opposite end of the spectrum. She struggled to fit in, and yet as the role was a promotion she wanted to do well and to succeed.

The challenge was not only how to survive the toxic environment, but how to maintain her authentic self and integrity. She knew the line she didn't want to cross and constantly checked in to make sure it hadn't been crossed and that she hadn't changed herself to fit in.

Research conducted by Maryam Kouchaki at the Kellogg School, Francesca Gino at Harvard and Adam Galinsky of Columbia University has found that chronic phoniness comes at a cost, because being inauthentic makes us feel immoral. 'We shouldn't overlook the psychological distress that comes with inauthentic behaviour,' Maryam suggested. 'Just as an immoral act violates widely accepted societal moral norms and produces negative feelings, an inauthentic act violates being true to oneself, and it can take a similar toll.'

When you stop being your authentic self it causes psychological distress, which can have ongoing emotional and physical ramifications. This behaviour may include feigning interest, laughing at your boss's jokes in order to get along or agreeing to things you privately disagree with. Worse still, when you spend too long in a negative and unpleasant environment you may well find that the behaviour of others starts to rub off on you!

An organisational culture that tolerates or encourages behaviour that is bordering on dodgy or downright unethical can see people behave in ways that are out of character. They begin to adopt behaviour that they wouldn't consider appropriate or ethical as they become acculturated to the accepted way of behaving in that workplace.

That's why the vision and principles exercise you did in chapter 2 is so important. It sets the line you won't cross at work. As soon as you put your toe across that line and behave in a way that's out of kilter with your value set, it becomes easier to cross the line even further ... until you reach the point where your integrity and reputation are thoroughly tarnished.

A former colleague was working in Hong Kong for a large investment company, and his boss asked him to do something he saw as unethical. He told me, 'There really was no choice to make. I knew if I followed his instructions and didn't raise the issue with management I'd have compromised my principles for his. I resigned on the spot.'

> A job isn't worth selling your soul or your values for, because once your integrity is gone it's hard to restore it.

On the other hand, maybe you don't connect with the organisation's culture or product/services. One of my clients works for an organisation where she doesn't connect with the product they sell. She satisfies herself that she hasn't sacrificed her principles because her work is focused on two values that matter to her—connecting with and developing people.

It's time for you to reflect, challenge yourself and check you haven't crossed that self-imposed line.

TIME OUT

- Are you clear about your line and comfortable you are not stepping over it?
- Are you being courageous and stepping into important conversations?
- Is the workplace culture positively impacting your thoughts and actions?
- Are you living true to your vision and principles and being your authentic self at work?
- Do you like the person you are when you are at work?

If you answered mostly 'yes', then your markers are largely on track. If you answered 'no', then I'd encourage you to think about whether you are okay with the impact the environment is having on you.

One of my clients who recently left a toxic work environment told me, 'I realised I no longer liked the person the environment had turned me into. It was time to go.'

> If your work environment is changing who you are, and you no longer like the person you see in the mirror, then you need to assess how much longer you should stay.

Sense check your reality

Before you do pull the pin, I'd encourage you to sense check your reality with a coach, trusted colleague, friend or partner. It's easy to be too hard on yourself, and too hard on other people.

I often find that when I talk things through with my husband, Craig, he helps me see the other person's perspective. By seeing their perspective, I am able to shift my interpretation of what's happened and to have more understanding and compassion. Often, too, in that moment I realise that their behaviour isn't about me or directed towards me—it's about them and how they feel.

As the Danish philosopher Søren Kierkegaard once said, 'Life can only be understood backwards; but it must be lived forwards.'

On the field

Raj worked with an awesome bunch of people, but his boss was less than effective. He lived in a bubble, quite unaware of the team's workload, happily chirping 'work–life balance everyone' as he pranced out the door at 5 pm, while everyone else stayed back to finish their work.

Raj figured out he couldn't change his boss, but he could make the most of the parts he liked — the work and the team he worked with. Sure, the boss's behaviour was annoying, but the other two elements compensated for this, making it a worthwhile trade-off.

You may not always like your boss, but what other aspects of the work make it worthwhile to stay? Consider what matters most to you and what you may be willing to trade off.

PART II

What to do if you ... MANAGE ONE

You are likely reading this section because you are a leader of leaders or, let's say, one of the big bosses. Your position is crucial because of the influence you have in designing and shaping the culture in your division or even your entire organisation. Your impact flows on to the other leaders who report to you, and their impact flows on to the employees who report to them. Talk about responsibility!

> If someone who reports to you is managing people ineffectively, then you have a problem, and it's up to you to fix it.

Study after study has demonstrated that you get better outcomes when employees feel valued, are treated well, and are working in a happy, healthy and thriving work environment. Yet too many people still feel like wage slaves working in soulless environments, disconnected from their teammates.

Poor leadership is costly. It impacts staff engagement, employee mental health and wellbeing, and individual and collective productivity. If people in the organisation aren't healthy, productive and engaged, organisational performance results will suffer. And it has a ripple effect on how your customers and clients are treated. The adage that 'happy staff equals happy customers' is true. If employees aren't cared for, they won't care about the outcomes.

But it's not all doom and gloom. There is real hope. The fact that you are reading this proves that. The annual Great Place to Work survey shows there are many awesome places to work (such as Salesforce, Cisco, Hilton and Mecca brands), where people come to work, have fun, connect and deliver amazing outcomes. These are cultures that are deliberately created because people like you make a point of making it happen.

In great organisations like these, the boss or leader of leaders isn't putting effort into the culture because they're forced to. They're doing it because they know the value it delivers. They make it their business to know what is happening on the ground, and they don't step over poor and ineffective leadership when it's displayed by their direct reports.

As William Shakespeare said, 'There is no darkness but ignorance'. Let's step into the light and create a great culture where you, your direct reports and all of your employees can thrive.

5

ASSESS THE SITUATION

Admiral Horatio Nelson, considered perhaps Britain's greatest naval commander, had a long and distinguished career culminating in his decisive victory over the heavier combined fleet of France and Spain at the Battle of Trafalgar in 1805.

Britain's main advantage over France during the Napoleonic Wars was its naval superiority. A central part of its strategy, therefore, was to use that power to blockade the French naval ports, frustrating Napoleon's invasion plans, and to cut off trade with France by other nations, such as Denmark, which had joined the Second League of Armed Neutrality, created to counter this threat to their trade.

After rounds of failed diplomacy, a British fleet was sent to Copenhagen to force Denmark's hand and potentially secure an alliance to prevent the Danish navy falling into Napoleon's hands. Entering the harbour, the British ships were met by a Danish–Norwegian fleet determined to defend the capital. At one point in the battle, Nelson's superior, the more cautious Sir Hyde Parker, worrying that his second-in-command was suffering huge losses, hoisted the signal for all ships to disengage.

Nelson chose to ignore this signal, claiming he didn't see it. He had ostentatiously raised his telescope to the eye that had been blinded eight years earlier at the Battle of Corsica. An hour later the Danish ships were in ruins, and victory was Nelson's. This is often attributed as the origin of the saying to 'turn a blind eye'.

Nelson was lucky! He got a good outcome. Parker was recalled in disgrace, while Nelson was promoted to command the fleet. But often turning a blind eye has less happy consequences. You may have set clear leadership standards, and yet your direct report is turning a blind eye to what's expected of them. Alternatively, it may be you who are turning a blind eye to what your direct reports are doing (or not doing). Sometimes there may be legitimate reasons for doing so, but when you knowingly ignore bad leadership behaviour, you need to own that and accept the consequences.

One of my favourite former bosses used to say, 'What you step over, you endorse'. If there is poor, inadequate, bad, toxic or ineffective leadership from one of your direct reports and you leave it untreated, you are endorsing that behaviour.

It's not enough to say, 'I didn't know', because if it's happening on your watch it's your responsibility to know.

When you are ignorant of the workplace and whether it's flourishing or floundering, you don't do yourself or your organisation any favours.

The root cause of many systemic organisational failures is the lack of a healthy culture. Not surprisingly, therefore, an organisation's culture is now considered a key indicator of its future profitability and performance.

US-based investment manager WCM Investment assesses a company's culture as part of their process of deciding who to invest with. In an interview with the *Australian Financial Review*, WCM's co-chief executive Kurt Winrich highlighted the difference between two of the biggest US retailers, Costco and Walmart. He attributed their difference in performance not to their business model, but to how they treat their employees.

Both companies operate as warehouse-style retailers, but Costco pays employees better, and offers medical benefits and other incentives, achieving sales of US$1200 per square foot, double that of Walmart. 'We finally concluded that culture was the difference,' he said. 'It was the way they treated their people.'

You are a leader of leaders, and with that comes both enormous power and great responsibility.

You are not just leading your direct reports; you are shaping and influencing how they lead their teams and therefore the culture that is being created across the work environment. Remember, many leaders are simply unaware of their leadership gaps. So it's up to you to support them to become better leaders. This starts with taking an honest look at yourself.

Check yourself

Improving the culture and increasing the effectiveness of the leaders in your team won't work if you are missing one key ingredient—YOUR LEADERSHIP! If you come up short there, then any critical feedback you offer your team leaders is likely to raise the accusation of 'the pot calling the kettle black'.

There are two aspects to this:

1. How can you call to account and coach your team on how to be better leaders if you aren't an exemplary leader? Quite simply, you can't because it will be seen as hypocritical, and consequently your advice and counsel will fall on deaf ears.
2. Employees at lower levels in the organisation are never going to tell you how they feel about their boss. Why? Because they won't trust you to do anything about it, given your own leadership performance. Also, they'll likely assume you know about it already and simply don't care.

For this to work, it's essential you are trustworthy, connected and respected, and that you role model leadership daily!

> Before you check the effectiveness of the leaders reporting to you, reality check the effectiveness of your own leadership.

Open your eyes

Now, let's say you're ready to move on. You're ready to assess what is really going on in the teams that are part of your function, division or organisation. It could be you think everything is going swimmingly… that is, until someone valued—an employee who reports directly not to you but to the leader you manage—suddenly resigns.

Some people are particularly skilled in the art of 'managing up', which means your direct report could be managing you! Alternatively, you could also have some amazing employees (like the one who just resigned) who make your direct report (their boss) look good to you.

So it's important to keep your eyes wide open and your ears tuned in.

It's easy to see what you want to see, or what someone else wants you to see. The leaders reporting to you will want to impress you, do well and show you they are delivering. This means they may be shielding you from their mistakes, inflating the good parts and downplaying the bad, or glossing over areas in which they don't excel.

It's also all too easy to hold fixed views on colleagues, especially if you have worked together for years or are on friendly terms. A strong bond may mean you are reluctant to see (or act) when their leadership isn't hitting the mark. Perhaps they are the superstar salesperson who always brings in revenue, so you don't want to risk losing them by addressing their questionable leadership behaviours.

Remember, what you say and do sets your leadership reputation, and ultimately shapes the workplace culture.

It's your responsibility to tune into the right frequency and maybe change the channel you are listening to.

Sense check weak signals

A great leader is alert to weak signals and to signs of discontent across their team. They'll dig, check and inquire into what might be going on to cause the rumbles and rumours, before acting with integrity and purpose.

Sense checking starts with informal and formal data sources:

- **Informal**. This is the feedback you may hear or see from your direct report's team members and peers, their executive assistant (if they have one), and suppliers or customers they deal with.
- **Formal**. This is hard data from engagement results, 360-degree feedback assessments, feedback from employee exit interviews and other performance metrics such as productivity, staff turnover, absenteeism, stress levels and any formal complaints.

Let's take a look at the informal sources first.

Informal sources

Watching what's going on isn't about having a network of moles who monitor and track every move your direct report makes. It's about being diligent and observant, and talking with people. It's about being available and present with both those leaders who report to you and those employees who report to them. This is what great leaders do. They put people at the centre of it all.

> Informal feedback can happen by chance, but for it to be regular and accessible you need to make a habit of talking with people.

Informal feedback involves:

- *walking the floor and getting a sense of the workplace culture and dynamics.* Are the energy levels high or low? Are people engaging and connecting with each other?
- *chatting with people throughout the organisation.* Ask them about their day and what they are working on. The more interested you are in them, the more they'll be willing to share.
- *attending your direct report's team meetings sometimes.* What's on the agenda? Does your direct report do all the talking or encourage team members to speak up? Is there good-natured banter and open discussion, or is the conversation reluctant and stilted?
- *having a regular schedule of leader-once-removed meetings.* These are one-on-one chats with your direct report's team members. Ideally, do it in a relaxed environment, such as over a coffee or at the local café. You want to find out how they are feeling, what's going on and what they need from you.
- *having regular one-on-one chats with your direct report.* These conversations help build rapport and connection, as well as offering opportunities to hear directly about their progress and where they'd like more support.

Someone else you will want to chat with is your direct report's executive assistant, if they have one. INSEAD Business School conducted research into the kinds of abuses of power executive assistants witness. Their report, 'The Secret Power in the Office', received responses from more than 200 executive assistants across 22 European countries. It found that 48 per cent of respondents said they knew of some form of serious misconduct by their boss over the past 12 months:

- 32 per cent identified waste or abuse of organisational resources
- 14 per cent saw activities that constituted a conflict of interest
- 13 per cent reported mishandling of confidential information
- 3 per cent witnessed theft and asset misappropriation.

In most cases, the executive assistants did not report the issue because it was either too much hassle or it felt unsafe to do so because their boss was involved.

Be careful, though!

> This isn't about getting people, who are usually incredibly loyal, to spy or turn on their boss and divulge their secrets.

You don't want to introduce Big Brother into your office so every move everyone makes is watched, monitored and assessed. That's stressful, unproductive and not a nice place to work, and it will backfire, sending issues underground. You want to create a culture of openness and transparency. This is about helping, not hindering; coaching, not criticising; supporting, not stressing out everyone involved.

Conversation etiquette

The feedback you receive from employees may not be clearly articulated. It often takes enormous courage for someone lower in the hierarchy to speak up, so they may be nervous and anxious. Don't discount a message that's delivered poorly or at the wrong time or place. As leadership experts Ronald Heifetz and Donald Laurie put it, '… buried inside a poorly packaged interjection may lie an important intuition that needs to be teased out and considered. To toss it out for its bad timing, lack of clarity, or seeming unreasonableness is to lose potentially valuable information.'

You need to establish rapport and trust. Over time, as that builds up and communication lines open, employees will be more willing to tell you what's going on for them.

In your leader-once-removed meetings, it's important to set the frame and tone for the conversation. Focus the meetings on better understanding their career aspirations, how they are being fulfilled and what they need to be their best at work.

The goal is healthy, productive conversations that generate insight, rather than a bitch-fest where the employee just downloads everything they don't like about their boss.

You mustn't inadvertently undermine your direct report's leadership by how you carry out these sessions. Be curious, interested and mindful of how you ask questions.

Use openers such as:

- 'I'm wondering ...'
- 'Can I sense check something with you?'
- 'Can I clarify ...?'
- 'What's your perspective on ...?'

Remember to be open to what you're hearing. This isn't about explaining why the employee might be wrong. You've got to be willing to listen to their point of view, even if it contradicts your own.

Of course, feedback can be malicious, and some of the information and stories you are told could be a product of personal agendas or conflicts. There are always at least two sides to every story.

Consider the informal feedback you receive from two angles:

1. What's the intent of the person providing the feedback? Is it helpful or unhelpful, good or not so good? Do they have a personal agenda?
2. What's the expertise or experience of the person offering the feedback? How qualified are they to provide their opinion?

It's a case of discern and learn:

- **Discern**. If you are worried about the intent and quality of the feedback, then dig deeper and ask lots of questions. Sift through the feedback and be alert to the fact that it may be self-serving or ill-advised.
- **Learn**. If the intent and quality seem sound, then ask lots of questions and be really interested in their feedback to see what more you can learn about their experience. Seek to understand where they are coming from, then reflect, listen to yourself and determine the best strategy to move forward (more on that in the next chapter).

Ideally, you're not getting occasional feedback from one person; you're getting feedback all the time from lots of people.

Remember, different employees look for different things in their leader, so you need to weigh up the comments you hear from different sources. It's that mix of sources and comments that helps you build an accurate picture of what's going on.

Look for warning signs

As you talk, connect and share with people across your teams, you'll start to get a feeling (weak or strong) for the nature and character of your leader's leadership. You may also sense clear warning signs that something is off kilter.

Here are 10 warning signs to be alert for:

1. **Inconsistent behaviour**. Notice how the leader (your direct report) behaves in front of you, when other people are around, and in meetings with their peers or team. Consider if their behaviour is consistent, or if it changes based on who is in room.
2. **It's always about them**. The leader never acknowledges the efforts of their team, always talks about themselves and what they need, and makes sure they always look good. It's about them winning and coming out on top.
3. **It's never their fault**. The leader is reluctant to admit mistakes and seeks to blame others to ensure there is little or no scrutiny on how they need to change or improve. Similarly, their team appears to struggle to regroup and learn when things go wrong.
4. **They won't compromise**. They are unwilling or find it very hard to change their mind, and seek always to get what they want, whether it's resources, rewards or approval of ideas. They rarely, if ever, compromise.
5. **They don't back themselves**. The leader is overly compliant and unwilling to back what they stand for, so they don't back their team and what they need.
6. **The leader's team is MIA**. You rarely engage with their team, and when you do the employees seem ill-informed and reluctant to talk to you. They seem to lack cohesion and focus, so you get a sense there is

no 'team'. Your direct report never delegates meetings (involving you or more senior stakeholders) to their team members.

7. **Concern for their team is missing**. When you ask about their team, the leader always merely insists everything is going well. They never ask for advice or help, and any issues you raise about their team are brushed aside.
8. **They play favourites**. The leader always promotes one person in the team over the rest, and delegates the good work or rewards only to that one person.
9. **They don't back their team**. Team members are rarely promoted, suggesting the leader may not be good at coaching and developing. Neither is the team diverse and inclusive, indicating the leader may only be hiring people who fit a certain mould.
10. **The team seems stuck**. The work isn't delivered to a high quality and standard, so there's lots of rework and long hours, which can be a sign of stress and poor leadership focus.

Warning signs are just that, and ideally they should be validated through your formal sources.

Formal sources

Formal sources of data help to validate what you are seeing or hearing informally.

Your access to formal data will depend on what your organisation collects, and what you are willing to invest time and money on. Most organisations have some form of annual or periodic staff satisfaction or engagement survey. These surveys can be a useful indicator of what is happening in teams, and whether the work environment is happy and healthy or a constant struggle and challenge.

Consider when the survey is taken though, because the results reflect how people feel at a specific point in time. Also, they aren't solely a reflection on the leader, but rather an indication of how the employee feels about the organisation, including its culture, systems, processes and remuneration frameworks.

I've seen situations where great leaders have received low team engagement results because the tools, systems and processes the employees used were clunky and cumbersome, frustrating many of the team.

What are most helpful are 360-degree feedback assessment tools. They aren't to be used as a weapon to decide whether or not to fire someone, but rather as an indicator to determine where the leader may need coaching and development support.

The idea of the 360-degree assessment can be traced back to the work of psychologists Joseph Luft and Harrington Ingham, who developed the Johari window in the 1950s. This technique was designed to help people better understand their relationship with themselves and others, to increase their personal growth and to build better relationships, as shown in figure 5.1.

A 360-degree feedback process involves multiple sources, ensuring that a variety of perspectives of the leader's performance and behaviours are captured. The aim is to source feedback from people who work directly with the leader, including their boss, peers, direct reports, and potentially customers, clients and suppliers too. The leader also completes a self-assessment.

You need to make sure there is an appropriate sample size, and the leader isn't just seeking feedback from people they think like them or will be nice about them.

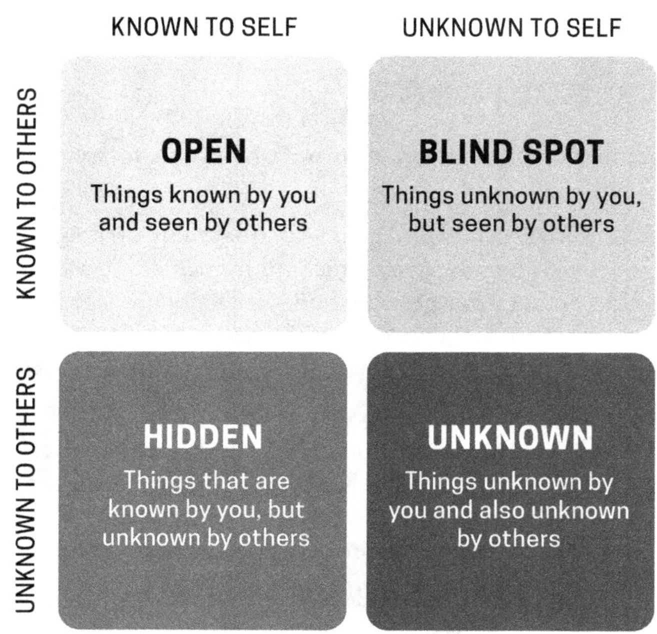

Figure 5.1: The Johari Window

The resulting report then reveals what is and isn't working, areas of strength and areas needing development. The most effective assessment tools enable you to segment the results so you can distinguish differences across different classes of respondents. This can be incredibly insightful as it highlights how a person can be viewed differently by their direct reports, their peers and you.

Other performance metrics, such as productivity, staff turnover, absenteeism, stress levels and any formal complaints lodged, will also help build the picture of what's playing out in the leader's team.

Ask before they go

Exit interviews with employees who are leaving the team or organisation are really helpful. However, be mindful of the circumstances under which they are leaving and whether this might affect the tenor or legitimacy of their comments.

Take time to prepare for the interview, and give the departing team member time to prepare as well.

In the interview you might ask questions such as these:

- What did you like most/least about your role?
- Did you have the resources, equipment and skills necessary to succeed in the role?
- If you could have changed one thing about your role, what would it have been?
- What did you learn about leadership while working in this role?
- When did you start considering leaving this role/organisation?
- How would you describe the organisation's/your team's culture?
- If you could change one thing in that culture, what would it be and why?
- Were you given constructive and regular feedback?
- Would you recommend this role to someone else?

These formal and informal sources will help you form a perspective of the person you are managing — their leadership strengths and weaknesses.

You need to sift through the information and be curious about what you are hearing and seeing, and what it could be telling you. If there's a big gap between what the leader is saying to you and what you are seeing or hearing from others, then it's time to ask why.

Uncover the root cause

This starts with a very simple question to the person you're managing: 'I want to ensure I am bringing out the best in your leadership, so what more do you need to be the best leader you can be?' This isn't just a question you ask if you think something is off track. It's also a great question to ask so you ensure everything *stays on track.*

Your goal is to have them sharing and reflecting on what is and isn't working for them. This may take some time, and it may need more than one conversation — indeed it may need many.

The aim is to uncover the root cause of the issues. Is it stress? Is it the culture? Are they in a role that doesn't bring out their best? Do they lack technical or professional skills? Do they not have the right team or enough resources? Are you not doing enough or perhaps unwittingly contributing to the problem?

For this to work, you need to be ready to accept that some responsibility for any problems may rest with you. Remember, your behaviour sets the standard. You can't expect your direct reports to meet higher standards than you do. If they don't feel empowered by you, they are less likely to empower their own team. If they feel micro-managed by you, then they are more likely to do the same with their team.

Research has demonstrated that followers tend to emulate the leadership behaviour they experience from their leaders. In fact, researchers at the Kelley School of Business found that 'the best predictor of follower aversive leadership — the use of threats and intimidation — was the aversive leadership of the designated leader'.

A joint study, conducted by Vanderbilt University, Cornell University and the University of Illinois, of 1527 full-time employees at 94 hotels across the United States and Canada found a positive correlation between middle managers' satisfaction with their senior managers and the line employees' satisfaction with their middle managers. It's a trickle-down effect. When senior leaders treat their direct reports badly, this dysfunction cascades down through the organisation.

It's critical, therefore, to check your own behaviour first.

TIME OUT

- How is your leadership behaviour contributing to your direct report's behaviour?
- Is it helping or hindering their progress?
- Are you putting too much pressure on them?
- Are your expectations about what can get done by when, given the resources and other work on the go, unreasonable?
- Are you spending enough time coaching and supporting them?
- What more can you do to encourage them to bring their best selves to work?

It's easy to say you want great leaders and a healthy team culture, but are you demonstrating and rewarding behaviour to promote it?

Sanity check

Adam Grant, an organisational psychologist at Wharton University, observed, 'When assholes win, it's because we let them get away with it. We let it happen when we build cultures that only prize individual achievements. We promote people who produce short-term results, ignoring the long-term damage they do.' He suggests that we fall into the trap of believing the myth that a person is indispensable, so keep them around even when they treat others like dirt.

You need to be clear about what you are rewarding and why, and the flow-on impacts to the behaviour of the leaders in your team.

Use table 5.1 (overleaf) to do a quick sanity check and see if you can spot areas where you are being inconsistent.

Table 5.1: sanity check your consistency

DO YOU SAY YOU WANT ...	BUT ACTUALLY REWARD ...
• a sustainable and flexible work environment and a happy healthy culture	• long hours, overtime and an 'always on' culture
• to put people first	• output, output, output
• teamwork	• individuals
• a safe workplace where people can be themselves	• a workplace where people conform and are compliant
• open and transparent communication	• people saying what you want to hear
• feedback on how you are progressing	• people saying nice things to you
• continuous improvement	• only surfacing the good news
• a collegiate environment where everyone advances and shares in the rewards	• an environment where it's all about you and your success
• responsible earning of profits?	• profit at all cost incentive structures?

It's useful to understand what drives and motivates your direct report. Are they extrinsically motivated—by pay, rewards or status? Or are they intrinsically motivated—by the internal satisfaction of seeing progress, learning and development?

How they are motivated will shape the choices they make in their leadership role. If it's all about the extrinsic rewards, you may find they are more likely to focus on their needs and making themselves look good. If their motivation is derived from within, you are more likely to see them considering needs beyond their own and striving for progress for the sheer pleasure of seeing positive impacts for others.

Culture doesn't fit

No doubt you'll have heard culture referred to as 'the way things are done around here'. It includes the unwritten rules of behaviour around what is acceptable and unacceptable.

As tribal creatures we notice what other people are doing, often adopting it as a standard behaviour to help us adapt to our surroundings. This process of acculturation can happen quickly as social cues are noticed and behaviours adopted so we feel like we belong to the tribe. A culture where behaviours are questionable can produce poor outcomes.

But it's not just that. Some cultures are fast-paced, ambiguous and complex, others more relaxed and creative. There are a myriad of different cultures, and different people thrive in different environments. Sometimes an environment simply isn't bringing out the leader's best.

TIME OUT

- How is the work culture impacting your direct report? Is it productive or unproductive?
- Does this work environment bring out their best?
- If not, what would need to change for them to be able to bring their authentic self to work?

They're out of their depth

One study, in the United States and Britain, looked at how workers are affected by their boss's technical competence. They did this in three ways, examining:

1. whether the supervisor could, if necessary, do the employee's job
2. whether the supervisor worked his or her way up inside the organisation
3. the supervisor's level of technical competence as assessed by their direct report.

They found that employees were far happier when they were led by a person with deep expertise in the core activity of the business—someone who understood their work and what they did. In fact, the impact of having a highly competent boss had the largest positive influence on an employee's level of job satisfaction.

Among American workers, having a technically competent boss was more important for employee job satisfaction than their salary, even when their salary was high. The researchers also discovered that when employees stayed in the same job but got a new boss, the employees' job satisfaction rose if that person was technically competent.

The theory known as the Peter Principle suggests that managers rise to the level of their own incompetence. One reason this happens is that we look at a person's performance in their current role, rather than looking at the skills they'd need in their future role.

In a study covering 214 organisations and 1500 employees in sales roles, the researchers found many cases of this phenomenon. The data suggested that the better sales representative a person was, the more likely they were to be promoted into management. However, this had negative outcomes for the salesperson's new team members.

A new manager's high sales performance before they got the promotion was associated with a 7.5 per cent decline in the sales performance of their new subordinates. By contrast, when the new manager's prior sales performance was relatively poor, there was a significant improvement in their new subordinates' performance.

Just because a person's output is good doesn't mean they are automatically going to be a good leader—yet. There may be other mitigating forces at play. The leadership problems may be the result of ingrained behavioural patterns or a temporary blip caused by an inability to cope with external pressures.

This isn't about making excuses for their behaviour. Rather, it is about being fair and kind and recognising that everyone is human and sometimes people aren't their best when overwhelmed by external pressures.

TIME OUT

- Are there events occurring in their personal life that are causing stress and distraction?
- Is there an unusually high volume of work and too many tight deadlines?
- Is there a resource shortfall that is creating pressure?
- Do they appear overworked, fatigued and stressed out?
- Are there organisational changes underway that are creating uncertainty?
- Are there other workplace changes that could be impacting their behaviour?
- Do they have the technical competence to do their role?

People who make the best bosses have a genuine desire to make the life of those around them better.

In the next chapter, we'll consider the options you have to better support your people and leaders.

On the field

Gabrielle, an executive managing a large team, had a niggling suspicion that something wasn't working with one of her direct reports but couldn't figure out what it was.

Together we used the '5 Whys' technique, which was developed by Toyota's founder, Sakichi Toyoda, to help work through cause and effect. The technique is so named because it's based on the idea of asking 'why' five times to get to the root cause of an issue.

In this scenario, her direct report had missed another client deadline, though as always offered an excuse that on the surface seemed plausible. The initial reason was conflicting priorities and workloads. Gabrielle wanted to find out the real cause, and using this technique she uncovered the following:

1. Why did they miss the client deadline?
   Because of conflicting priorities and workloads.
2. Why are there conflicting priorities and workloads?
   Because they haven't got a prioritisation schedule in place.
3. Why don't they have a prioritisation schedule in place?
   Because they don't spend time with their team planning and managing workflow.
4. Why don't they spend time with their team doing this?
   Because they don't have a regular operating rhythm of meetings and daily interactions that help them prioritise and manage workloads.
5. Why don't they have a regular operating rhythm to manage workload?
   Because the leader doesn't spend enough time with his team.

In applying this technique, Gabrielle was able to discuss and validate with the direct report what was going on and to work through steps to address it. It's important always to look beyond your first conclusion to remove any invalid assumptions.

6
STRATEGISE
THE PATH FORWARD

There's nothing worse than finding out that one of your star team members has let you down. That's just what happened in 1998 when Stephen Glass, then considered a journalist superstar, was exposed as a fraud. Turns out most of his stories were either wholly or partially fabricated—*eek!*

Glass, who was still in his twenties, was a staff writer for one of America's most respected publications, *The New Republic*, and freelanced for *Harper's*, *Rolling Stone* and *George*. His lies started to unravel in May when *The New Republic* published 'Hack Heaven', a story detailing the exploits of a 15-year-old who'd hacked a major software company.

Fearing they'd been scooped, the online Forbes Digital Tool (now Forbes.com) started digging around. They discovered no evidence of the existence of the company described in the article, or of the hacker or the legislation cited.

Glass had gone to extreme lengths to cover his tracks, creating a fake website for the company and business cards for his sources. He even had his brother pose as a company executive.

It is hardly surprising that the story became the subject of a movie, *Shattered Glass*, released in 2003. In a scene after the fraud has been exposed, Glass (played by Hayden Christensen) asks his editor, Charles 'Chuck' Lane (played by Peter Sarsgaard), 'Are you mad at me?' (*Oh my god, wouldn't you be?*)

His fraud damaged not only himself, but his colleagues and the *entire* publication. *The New Republic* eventually acknowledged that 27 of the 41 pieces written by Glass during his three-year tenure had been fabricated. This wasn't a case of plagiarism, but of lies, deception and fantasy. How on earth did he get away with it for so long?

A detailed exposé in *Vanity Fair* reported that Glass's first editor at *The New Republic*, Michael Kelly, 'never wavered in his support for the cub reporter he had helped catapult into the big leagues', and when Kelly was confronted with accusations of fabrication in Glass's work he responded not by questioning Glass but by sending angry letters to the offended parties, dismissing the complaints as 'meritless'.

Why did Glass do it? The same article proposed pressure to perform, stress, overwork and an 'improvised adventure of the mind' as contributing factors.

What's also interesting is that there had been rumours and speculation for years about the veracity of his work, yet it took determined digging by an outside publication to expose what was really going on.

Ignorance is bliss — until it bites you on the nose.

As the boss's boss, a leader of leaders, it's way too easy to ignore what is happening right under your nose, and to hope (and perhaps pray) it goes away or miraculously just fixes itself. It won't!

So regardless of what you've heard or discovered is going on (hopefully, nothing as bad as outright fraud), you have to take ownership of it and do something about it.

Reality bites

It's easy to sit back and think, 'That would never happen to me'. Sadly the statistics suggest otherwise.

A study by researchers from the University of Central Florida's College of Business found that a person considered a top performer was much more likely to have bullying behaviour overlooked by their manager. What's more, often the victims of that behaviour were themselves, quite unfairly, seen as the bullies and received lower job performance evaluations as a result of being victimised.

The study's co-author, Shannon Taylor, an Associate Professor of Management, attributed this flawed decision making to cognitive bias. He explained it in terms of 'the halo effect, in which positive attributes mask negative traits, or the horn effect, in which one negative attribute casts a person in a completely negative light'.

I've seen senior leaders excuse poor behaviour because a team member is bringing in huge sales and big customer deals, or because they're 'a mate'. I'm sure you've experienced something similar.

The Roman philosopher Seneca said, 'It is not because things are difficult that we do not dare; it is because we do not dare that things are difficult.' Your decision on the best strategy to take can be challenging and will depend on whether the root cause sits with you, them or the environment in which you work:

1. **You**. You may need to read Part III of this book so you can address the impact you are having as a leader and work out how and where you need to lift your game. As well, you may need to spend more time coaching, or address any structural issues that are contributing to your direct report's behavioural gaps.
2. **Them**. You will need to work through a series of steps to uncover their awareness of the gap, their leadership perspective, their willingness to change, what you can do to support them, and how prepared you are to invest that time and energy.
3. **Environment**. You should consider what aspects of the environment can be changed or what actions you can take to help your direct report cope better with the work environment.

It is likely that your way forward will involve all three elements, so your strategy pathway will be multi-pronged.

Now you may be thinking, isn't one of my options to move them on or fire them? No, not yet. You need to be fair and you need to give them time to improve. The only caveat to that is if the behaviour you have uncovered is illegal (which is beyond the scope of this book), in which case you are in a different ball game and you'll need to consult with HR and legal to work out what to do pronto.

What to do if it's YOU

You play two roles in this relationship dynamic:

1. **Starring role**. Your leadership must shine through at all times to all your direct reports and their employees.
2. **Supporting role.** You are the leader's leader, and with that comes the responsibility to coach and support them in a way that enables them to reach their leadership potential.

You need to identify what you are prepared to do to support the leader's leadership journey.

It may be that you will have more regular one-on-ones, offer more regular feedback or provide them with more development opportunities.

TIME OUT

- What do they need from you to elevate their leadership growth?
- Are you spending enough time with them?
- Are there other changes you can make to help them grow?

Take a moment to reflect and write down the top five things you are prepared to stop, start or continue doing that will help them become a better leader. After you've done that, ask yourself the following questions:

- Is that likely to be enough, or will you need to step up and do more?
- How committed are you to helping them succeed?
- Do you have any hidden agendas? For instance, are you secretly hoping they won't make the grade?

If you are not genuinely interested in helping the leader succeed in changing, then they are doomed to fail, because no matter what they do it won't be enough.

Remember, you can't expect the leader to change overnight. Behavioural change takes time, and they'll need to focus on a couple of areas at a time. That's why it's so crucial to be targeted in your approach and to focus specifically on the behaviours that are likely to have the most positive impact.

People are goal-oriented, and motivation is sustained by seeing progress. Encourage them to test and learn. Provide opportunities and stretch assignments where they can practise new skills, then give them the space and time to reflect and refine their approach so their new way of leading is embedded both cognitively and behaviourally.

What to do if it's THEM

Everything starts with a conversation, or in this case a series of coaching conversations (more on how you do that in the next chapter).

These conversations are focused on uncovering their level of awareness, how willing they are to face into the feedback, and their readiness to take the necessary steps to change, develop and enhance their leadership.

> You can't make this matter to them; for it to take effect, they have to want to change and be willing to put in the effort.

Many years ago one of the leaders in my team refused to hear constructive feedback. She viewed her work as perfect and her leadership as exemplary. Such a person can on the surface appear uncoachable because they are so reluctant to change. With patient and persistent counselling, however, she started to see her behaviour in another light, along with what could be cultivated and honed into real leadership.

So be prepared to put in the effort. This is rewarding and necessary, but it can also be hard and thankless work.

There are five crucial stages in this process:

1. **Journey**. Understand their leadership journey to date, and what's shaped how they see the world and their role as a leader. Share your perspective on leadership, and how you've grown and changed as a leader. Get their input and perspective on their current leadership growth and development areas (what they do well and not so well, for example), and determine to what extent they are

unconsciously incompetent, consciously incompetent or consciously competent.

It helps if you understand their context and mental frame of reference. Perhaps they've never been exposed to good leadership before. If they've never had a good role model, they are likely to struggle with understanding how to be a good leader.

2. **Vision**. Talk to them about their leadership vision to discover what type of leader they want to be. This will help them set the leadership goals they aspire to achieve.

   If they struggle with this idea, reading Part III of this book will really help them. Encourage them to write down their leadership vision, using the activity outlined in chapter 10.

3. **Mindset**. Uncover what type of mindset they are applying to their leadership work. Fixed or growth? Feast or famine? Being a leader is challenging, and it helps to apply a growth and feast mindset.

   If they are unwilling to admit they need to change and take steps to improve, it's likely they are approaching the situation with a fixed mindset. If that's the case, there's work to do helping them confront the reality of their situation.

4. **Action plan**. Identify the key areas of behavioural change required and what specific actions they can take to make that happen. Get them to be as specific as possible. It's easier for them to execute change when they identify the steps to take every day to achieve their leadership vision.

   As part of this plan you may need to set short- and long-term goals, depending on whether issues have arisen because of temporary blips caused by workplace stress (or something else), or if there are more ingrained behavioural patterns that need to be addressed and altered.

   You'll also want to identify the specific support you can offer, which may be internally or externally sourced:

   - **Internal support**. As their leader you'll provide this through coaching and mentoring, as well as support from HR, and internal training and development programs.
   - **External support**. This will entail an investment in the services of an executive coach to provide support and challenge, or external training and development programs.

Remember, often you can offer the best support by being available, interested in them, and providing regular in-the-moment feedback and coaching.

Their goals and supporting action plan should be documented — and not just for legal reasons, but because when something is written down it's harder to forget. The writing process helps with their next step — establishing commitment.

Encourage them to read Part III of this book, which outlines a series of ideas and strategies they can implement to help them reach their leadership potential.

5. **Commitment**. You need to understand how committed they are and the level of energy they are prepared to devote to this.

   Donald Sull and Charles Spinosa examined over a decade how promises are kept and broken in organisations. They found that promises are kept only about 50 per cent of times. What constituted an effective promise — that is, one that was most likely to be delivered — had five attributes. They are:

   - **Public:** Promises that are made visible, monitored and completed in public are more binding. This is because it's harder for the employee to forget, whether deliberately or unintentionally.

     Consider if there are ways the leader can safely share their development goals more broadly than just with you. It can be a powerful statement if they have the courage to share their development focus with their team, because it demonstrates a real commitment to change.

   - **Active:** The commitment should be developed collaboratively, with the involvement of other people connected to the issue.

     In the context of your scenario, this means you need to play your part in working with the leader collaboratively to develop their goals. To be effective, it can't be a one-way process.

   - **Voluntary:** They are not coerced into agreeing to something they don't want to do. A person is more likely to follow through if they freely entered into the arrangement.

     Consider what mechanisms are in place to ensure the leader is really buying into the process and isn't just saying what they think you want to hear.

- **Explicit:** All parties to the promise know who will do what by when. You play a role, and they play a role.
- **Mission-based:** The critical need for this promise is clearly articulated. Each party understands the rationale and importance of the request and invests time in the mission.

This last element connects directly to why the leader needs to spend time considering and articulating their leadership vision and must be aware of the consequences that will arise should behaviour change fail to occur.

These stages may not happen in a neat, linear fashion. You may find you go back and forth on elements as the conversation progresses, but make sure all stages are covered.

While it's critical for your direct report to feel supported through the process, they also need to acknowledge the need for improvement, and accept that you will hold them accountable for the effectiveness and impact of their behaviours.

Where possible, look at what options you have to implement behaviour-based KPIs and group-based success metrics. If the leader's incentives and rewards are all about outputs, and not about the behaviour they use to secure those outputs, then the equation is out of balance and you are ultimately rewarding the poor behaviour.

Balance the 'how' they do it and the 'what' they deliver.

There may also be performance hurdles you can put in place to assist the process.

Establish the consequences that could occur if there is no improvement. These may range from their being held back from further promotions within the organisation to—in cases of serious misconduct—formal performance monitoring and ultimately termination. Before that ultimate step can occur, however, the behavioural expectations must have been clearly and precisely articulated.

What to do if it's the ENVIRONMENT

As the big boss, you play a role in shaping your organisation's culture. However, you can't control everything, and yet when something isn't working it's easy to become consumed and to focus your energy on things you have little or no ability to influence.

In these types of situations, it's helpful to use an extended version of an approach outlined by Stephen Covey in *The 7 Habits of Highly Effective People*.

Think about the leader and the working environment, and ask yourself:

1. What can you be concerned about—but have little or no control over?
2. What can you be concerned about—but have the ability to influence or change?
3. What can you control?

In reality, the only thing you can control is your own thought processes, behaviour and actions. You can't control your leaders or employees. You can, however, influence and change the team environment and, depending on where you sit in the organisation's hierarchy, you will have influence over other aspects of the culture.

You can't force someone to fit a certain mould. Different people thrive in different environments. If the work environment is unpredictable and fast-paced and they prefer a more stable, slow-paced environment, then it may not be the place for them.

But if the workplace is one where people are made to feel excluded because of race, background, gender, age or any other factors, then you are facing an ethical and legal liability and you'll want to get your skates on and change the culture.

It's neither reasonable nor healthy to expect someone to change who they are to conform to a certain culture. And you shouldn't strive to have a team where everyone thinks and acts in the same way.

When everyone in the team shares similar backgrounds, experiences and thought processes, this homogeneity has flow-on impacts on how decisions are made. The more alike people are, the more likely they are to think along the same lines and the less room there is for debate, discernment and disagreement.

Diverse teams make better decisions. Research shows that diverse groups outperform more homogeneous groups not because of an influx of new ideas, but because diversity triggers more careful processing of the information that's discussed.

You need an environment that is both diverse and inclusive. As the leader of leaders, you may need to work on making the leader feel and be more included and part of the team.

TIME OUT

- Do you respect diversity or expect everyone to be the same?
- Do you ensure everyone in the team feels included, or do you play favourites?

What does this tell you about what you need to do differently to better create an environment where everyone can be their best?

While you can observe the culture and how it operates, there will be aspects that you can miss. As part of your action planning with your direct report, ask them about the culture and their perception of it. What aspects of the culture help them or hinder them? Then jointly look at strategies and actions you can implement to help them adapt to the culture or, where possible, adapt the culture to better suit them.

That's what we'll look at in more detail in the next chapter.

On the field

Penelope had a large and growing team and increasing expectations from internal and external stakeholders. She felt under pressure and needed her senior leadership team to play their part and deliver. Cracks in the team started to appear, and performance dropped. Her immediate reaction was to look to her direct reports to work out what needed to change, and she started to investigate restructuring options.

As we worked through the situation, it became apparent that the increasing pressure had shifted her leadership style and the pressure was getting fed down the system, creating challenges for her team.

Penelope recognised the first change that was needed was for her to accept responsibility for the environment she was creating. From there, she was able to set the right support, processes and behaviours to allow her direct reports and team to flourish.

It was a perfect example of the organisational pressure chamber in action, and of how finding the release valve needs to start at the top.

7
ACT
WITH PURPOSE

Charles Dickens' classic novel *A Christmas Carol*, published in 1843, tells the story of a mean-spirited old man, Ebenezer Scrooge. It's Christmas Eve and Scrooge is visited by the ghost of Jacob Marley, his former business partner, who warns him to change his miserly, tight-fisted ways or suffer the consequences. He tells Scrooge, 'No space of regret can make amends for one life's opportunity misused.'

'Bah, humbug,' retorts Scrooge, who pays little heed to the warning, so he continues to be haunted. First, the Ghost of Christmas Past appears to remind him of his early life. Scrooge is forced to revisit the scene where his then fiancée, Belle, dumps him because he loves money more than her. 'I have seen your nobler aspirations fall off one by one,' she admonishes him, 'until the master passion, gain, engrosses you.'

Next, the Ghost of Christmas Present appears to help him see that joy isn't about money, but about love, friendship and family. Finally, the Ghost of Christmas Yet to Come offers him a glimpse of the future: if he doesn't change his ways, Scrooge will die a sad, lonely and despised man.

These revelations of his character, actions and priorities and the lens through which he views the world shake him so deeply it compels him to change his ways. On Christmas morning Scrooge wakes up determined to be a better, kinder man.

While you're not going to dress up in a white sheet and rattle chains at night, your task is essentially the same as that of the three ghosts. Donning your leadership coaching hat, your aim is to help your leader see themselves through the three lenses of past, present and future.

1. **Past**. Have them assess what has influenced their leadership journey and their leadership expectations.
2. **Present**. Help them to determine the current state of their leadership and what needs to shift.
3. **Future**. Guide them towards setting their leadership vision, which articulates the leader they want to be, and support them as they put in place practices to bring that to life.

In the words of William Wordsworth: 'Life is divided into three terms—that which was, which is, and which will be. Let us learn from the past to profit by the present, and from the present, to live better in the future.'

Enter the arena

In chapter 3, I mentioned Dr Brené Brown's idea, developed in her book *Dare to Lead*, of 'arena moments' or moments of courage. This is a perfect way to describe the coaching conversations you now need to have with your direct report, where you will get them to discover and reflect and will hold them to their commitment to change.

Thinking about entering the arena can trigger a whole raft of negative emotions: fear, self-doubt, comparison, anxiety, uncertainty, even shame. It's natural to feel a mix of emotions. It's what makes us human. At times like this you can be tempted to do what Brené calls 'armour up'.

We do this in one of three ways—by:

1. **moving away**—withdrawing, hiding or not sharing who we are and how we feel
2. **moving towards**—seeking to appease and please others
3. **moving against**—being aggressive and using power to get what we want.

We hold back being ourselves, sharing our thoughts and ideas or having the tough conversations because we worry about how people may react.

When we worry about a conversation—whether to have it, how it will unfold and what the reaction will be—we often look to people sitting around the arena for acceptance and validation. We may look to the people in what Brené calls the 'cheap seats'—the people who won't ever get into the arena, but who are comfortable hurling abuse and being critical. Or we may look to the 'box seats'—the people who have power and whom we want to impress.

In your situation, the people in the cheap seats may be your peers or other people at work connected with your direct report, while your boss or your board are likely to occupy the box seat. For example, if you've worked out that part of the leader's problem stems from a leadership deficiency from you, this can be hard to admit, while if they are well connected across the organisation you may worry about blow-back if you try to address their leadership gaps.

But you can't walk away from this.

To secure results you need to back yourself, empathise with the leader, and face the challenge with courage.

Get ready to be real

Real conversations are at the heart of real relationships. This is a valuable opportunity to deepen and strengthen your team dynamics and performance. 'Winging it' won't work. Trying to ad-lib through a process of addressing issues means you've gone into the conversation unprepared. You haven't thought about what you need to cover and why, how the conversation may progress, how you will respond or your desired outcome.

This makes it all too easy for the conversation to drift and lose focus. Worse, if the conversation starts to get heated, you'll either step back to avoid confrontation, or end up throwing petrol on the fire, escalating it into conflict.

To be fully prepared, thoughtful and in control of what you say and how you react, use this three-step process:

1. Plan.
2. Deliver.
3. Reflect.

Let's look at each step now.

Step 1: Plan

First, think through the conversation. What's on the table for discussion? What is your desired outcome? Do you have any concerns, assumptions or preconceived ideas about how the conversation may progress? Have you raised the issue with them before, and if so, how did they react?

Then consider what your direct report's desired outcome may be and how they are likely to feel about the conversation. Will this conversation surprise them? How have they reacted when you've raised issues in the past? What is their level of awareness about their leadership gaps?

> If you care about the conversation you will enter into it with good intent, a genuine interest in your direct report and a desire to achieve a mutually beneficial outcome.

This means you'll strive to avoid any judgement, assumptions or preconceived ideas, and be curious, questioning, and eager to clarify and understand. Remember, how you frame the conversation will anchor it. It's important to avoid using 'us' and 'them' language, which can be seen as adversarial.

Consider the timing and make sure you are mentally prepared for it. Don't conduct difficult conversations when you (or your direct report) may be tired, hungry or stressed. Pay attention to the little things — location, whether it's best to hold the conversation onsite or offsite, noise levels, the need for privacy and any factors that could cause distraction. Ideally, have the conversation face to face as it is easier to build rapport and connection when you are in the same room.

Also, be fair. In many cases you will want to have a series of conversations with them. The first one could be short, because it's about setting the intention of the conversations and giving them time to consider their perspective.

If the conversation is set up badly and they feel ambushed and under threat, it is less likely to have a productive outcome. If your intent is to help them reach their leadership potential, then set the conversation framework and approach to support that intent.

This isn't the Spanish Inquisition: your intent is not to judge and pass sentence on them.

TIME OUT

- What are the biggest hurdles that will prevent this conversation from being successful?
- What are the biggest opportunities in this conversation?
- How much do you care about the outcome of the conversation?

Step 2: Deliver

Be mindful and fully present throughout the conversation. This isn't a one-way monologue. Listen and then probe, clarify, validate, normalise and make them feel heard. Notice what is going on for them and how they are reacting, while at the same time being aware of what is going on for you and how you are reacting.

When they don't feel heard they'll either withdraw from the conversation or find ways to destabilise or disrupt it.

By contrast, when a person feels heard they feel valued, like they matter to you. This is because they know their point of view has been considered and that you're interested not only in what they have to say, but in them.

This means you listen to the leader with compassion and empathy, ask questions and seek to clarify what you've heard before sharing your ideas or proposing a solution. In doing this you are acknowledging how they feel and taking the time to recognise their needs as important. You may not agree with what they are saying, but you respect their right to voice their perspective.

Give them space to process the conversation. If they think they are doing an awesome job and this is the first time they've heard otherwise, it shouldn't be surprising if they are defensive, withdrawn or reluctant to hear your perspective.

Be careful of reacting to their reaction. It's important to challenge your immediate response to what they are saying. An instant, reactive comeback is usually unwise and has the potential to harm the relationship further. A considered response indicates you are genuinely curious about what's happening, and what may have triggered their reaction. Then take the time to respond mindfully, always keeping focused on your intent and desired outcome.

Before you end each conversation check in on how they are feeling and ensure they know they matter to you and you want them to reach their full potential. Be clear on the next steps and what actions need to be taken — by you and the leader. You may want to have written some notes so you can track the conversations and commitments made.

TIME OUT

- What commitments were made in the conversation — by you and by your direct report?
- What are the next steps?

Step 3: Reflect

After the conversation, take the time to reflect on how it went. Consider your level of preparation, how it unfolded, how you and they reacted, whether the outcome was in line with your expectations, how you felt at the end of the conversation, and what you would do differently next time.

It really helps if your direct report also employs reflective practices as part of this process, so encourage them to take time out for this.

TIME OUT

- Did you achieve your desired outcome?
- If so, how? If not, why not?
- What would you do differently next time?

Ready the field for progress

Progressing your direct report and their leadership is not a single, one-off conversation or event. It's a series of conversations and events. It requires you to offer ongoing support, coaching and encouragement, to notice how they are going and to check in on their progress.

You play your part and they play theirs. It's about being the best leader of leaders you can be, and in turn motivating and inspiring them to do their very best work. This means investing time and energy!

Each of you plays a role in making this work — and work well.

Get ready to connect rather than disconnect. Step forward rather than turn away. Care deeply about the outcome, rather than having no more than a shallow interest. And enjoy it, because coaching people to reach their potential is a privilege, not a chore!

As part of this process, you need to take action to create a safe work environment. A psychologically safe environment is critical for high-performing teams to thrive. This is an environment in which everyone feels secure and included.

Amy Edmondson, Professor of Leadership and Management at Harvard Business School, highlights three steps you can take to create this environment at work.

1. Set the stage

This is about framing the work and ensuring everyone is on the same page. You need to establish common goals, clarity on challenges, and expectations on how you will deal with failure and uncertainty.

The team creates a shared understanding of what's at stake, why it's important and who is involved. They confirm the dependencies and connections across the team, and the criticality of continuous learning.

Your action: Ensure you have clear goals, responsibilities and ways of working together. How are you creating clarity rather than confusion about work, deadlines, dependencies and challenges?

2. Invite participation

For this to work, you need to be curious, humble and open to ideas, to have a growth mindset and to recognise you don't have all the answers. You ask questions, listen and use established mechanisms for facilitating discussions and gathering input from your team members. The point of this step is to ensure you have created the confidence in your team for them to share their ideas.

Your action: Check you are creating an environment in which questions can be asked and conversations are facilitated. What established forums and mechanisms are in place for idea sharing and collaboration? In what ways can leaders and employees each voice their ideas and concerns?

3. Respond productively

This all fails if you (the leader of leaders) don't respond well to the messages you hear or when your team takes risks. You need to praise people for their efforts and remove the stigma that is often attached to failure by focusing on learnings and growth. Lastly, establish processes to deal with times when there are clear and repeated violations of standards. This is about upholding the team's values, and this only works if the boundaries are clear and set in advance. The point of this step is to ensure the team is oriented towards continuous learning.

Your action: Check you have established clear standards and a learning culture. What actions have you implemented to create a psychologically safe work environment? How are you fostering genuine trust and care across the team?

> As the leader of leaders, your actions matter just as much as your direct report's actions.

When you are inconsistent and unreliable and your processes aren't clear, the rest of your team will see a failure to act as an indication that there are no clear standards or that they are inconsistently applied. That will impact how they feel, what they say and don't say to you, and subsequently how they behave and how much they trust you.

On the other hand, when you maintain fair processes, which are standardised and consistently applied, along with clear feedback mechanisms and established consequences for not meeting the standard, your team will trust that action is being taken.

Sometimes it feels easier to restructure and move a leader who isn't performing, than to invest the time in talking with them about their leadership gaps and working with them to help close them. That's not fair, nor is it kind and compassionate. Some leaders simply don't know they aren't performing well. From experience, there is nothing more rewarding than coaching a manager and watching them turn into the leader they can be.

It's your job to help them identify the gaps, then to help them close those gaps.

On the field

Chris, a senior executive in the services sector, had just taken on a senior leadership role and consequently inherited an established team. There was one leader in the team (let's call him TJ) who had a troubling reputation—having been characterised as difficult and ineffective. Chris was encouraged by the outgoing boss, his peers and HR to use the opportunity to restructure and move TJ on.

Chris wasn't comfortable acting without first providing TJ with the opportunity to demonstrate his capabilities. We talked through options and how to approach the situation, and decided the best approach was to be direct. He spent time with TJ, learning about his background, interests, leadership style and areas of concern. As he did this, he gradually uncovered what wasn't working.

Part of it was a lack of self-awareness, and part of it was that TJ felt unsupported by his previous boss. Consequently, he didn't raise questions or reach out for help. Chris and TJ worked through what needed to change, and with coaching support his leadership style shifted.

Over a period of 12 months, TJ went from being the laggard in the team to one of its top performers. Chris also generated incredible commitment and loyalty from TJ because he recognised the care and commitment that had been invested in helping him succeed.

When change happens, it's not just the person who changes who benefits.

8 REFLECT ON OUTCOMES

When you watch a sports team on the field, in the water or in whatever other domain they are performing, it's easy to see when they are in sync — connected, cohesive and collaborating as a team — and when they are disconnected, disorganised and dysfunctional.

When you analyse what makes them strong, it's unlikely that terms such as vulnerability, mindfulness and gratitude will top your list. Yet some teams are now starting to embrace these ideas as part of their coaching regime.

Here's a perfect example.

For Australian Football League (AFL) team the Richmond Football Club (known as the Tigers), 2016 was a disastrous year. They won only eight games (with 14 losses), which was a marked decline from 2015 when they won 15 games (with seven losses). Commentators faulted them for lacking form and substance, and there was much speculation around changes of coach, captain and line-up.

Embracing the work of Dr Brené Brown, the club built leadership and team practices that made it safe for the team to share, care and connect at a deeper level. For example, from early in the pre-season the club ran 'Hardship, Highlight, Hero' (HHH) sessions. In these group conversations each team member took a turn at sharing something highly personal to them — a story about a hero, hardship or highlight drawn from their own life.

During these sessions the club's coach, Damien Hardwick, shared a personal story, to be followed by the captain, Trent Cotchin, and other senior leaders. Their goal was to role model what it meant to be vulnerable and emotional and to trust one another.

As Richmond player Bachar Houli put it, 'You don't share something that is personal if you don't have the trust, and that is something that every player has done … There was emotion, because you're sharing something unique to yourself to your family, which we are here at the Richmond football club.'

This work is credited with creating deeper connections and trust, which translated into improved on-field performance. The Tigers went on to win the 2017 AFL Premiership, the 2018 minor premiership and the 2019 AFL Premiership, with an 89-point win over their grand final rivals Greater Western Sydney (GWS) Giants.

Winning the game wasn't a solo effort. Each individual had a role to play, but it was the sum of these parts that produced their on-field success. Dissecting their 2019 Premiership win, commentators said every member had a 'significant impact on this grand final'. The team's newfound strength meant 'this lot don't get spooked by tardy starts. They back their system. They back their talent. They trust one another. They're strong and they're bold.'

It's the same with your team.

> You need each individual to be their best if you want your team to be their best.

That means you might have to make hard decisions about who to coach, who to bench and who to trade.

Should they stay or go?

You've spent a great deal of time in this part assessing and understanding the effectiveness of the person who reports to you, their leadership style and where they can improve, as well as strategising ways to coach them through the process and have tough conversations to get a good outcome. While you'll be monitoring their progress throughout, after a reasonable period of time you'll want to make a more deliberative assessment of their progress.

There is no hard and fast rule on what should be considered 'a reasonable period of time'. It will differ based on a raft of circumstances, including their commitment to change, the complexity of the operating environment and their level of experience. It may be four, six or 12 months.

If you are leaving it any longer than 12 months, it's likely you are avoiding the decision. If you do anything too early, you aren't giving the leader time to improve. Fairly quickly, though, you will want to be confident that they are putting in the effort to try to change.

> It's a judgement call. Remember, be kind and be fair — always!

Although this isn't just about being kind and fair to them. A leader who isn't performing to the required standard can undermine you, their peers, their team and other parts of the organisation.

When you spend more time managing and coaching this one person, it can sometimes be to the detriment of the other leaders in your team. Those leaders, in turn, can feel resentful and frustrated because they feel this person is letting the team down while sucking up all your time and energy.

It's your role to coach and help this leader grow and develop. If you see little or no progress, however, then you have a tough decision to make.

Double check the data

We all apply filters in our interpretation of events and people, and this impacts how we feel, think and ultimately act. So as you undertake this reflection it will help to have a sounding board, someone who will hold up a mirror to you and challenge your interpretation and assessments.

You must be objective and fair when assessing the leader's progress and impact, which requires you to sense check how you are feeling and what you are thinking.

You'll have been regularly checking in with the leader's team and observing the leader in action as you have been doing this work. You will also have encouraged the leader to provide feedback on how they feel they are progressing.

If you've had them complete a 360-degree feedback assessment, and providing at least 12 months have passed, you might conduct another assessment to obtain objective evidence of progress. You could also look at the indicators and data points (such as turnover and productivity) outlined in the earlier chapters to see what's shifted.

In checking all the data points, consider what changes (if any) you have noticed and the impact those changes have had. Note what deliberate actions the leader has taken to shift their leadership behaviour, and whether their leadership gap is closing or widening.

TIME OUT

- Is the leader better, the same or worse with respect to their leadership behaviours?
- In which areas have they improved or not improved, and why?
- Where is further improvement needed, and why?
- Do they need more time to adjust?
- Do the strategies deployed need more time to bear fruit?
- Do the strategies need to change?
- Do you need to step up and do more to help?

It's not enough just to note if there has been improvement; you need to understand what has or hasn't driven the change.

After weighing up all those factors, you can then assess if enough improvement has been made.

Is enough enough?

When asking the question 'should they stay or go?', you need to consider the leader's level of readiness and willingness to change, along with the effort they are putting in. You also need to reflect on the amount of effort you are putting in to generate the level of improvement you are seeing.

This conjunction of factors is illustrated in figure 8.1.

To work out where your direct report currently sits, ask yourself some quick questions.

On *change acceptance*:

1. Have they willingly taken on board your performance feedback?
2. Have they acted on that feedback?

3. Have they shown genuine attempts to improve?
4. Have they put in the required level of effort?

If you answered 'no' to any of these questions, the leader is likely taking an 'intractable' approach to the challenge. If you answered 'yes' to all the questions, they are likely taking an 'adaptable' approach.

On *level of effort*:

1. Have they started to improve?
2. Are you comfortable with the amount of time you are spending coaching them?
3. Is that level of effort in line with your expectations, given the amount of progress made?
4. Is the focus required from you to help them shift their behaviour sustainable?

If you have answered 'no' to any of these questions, then the leader's impact on you and your time is likely to be 'intense'. If you answered 'yes' to all the questions, then their impact on you and your time is likely to be 'manageable'.

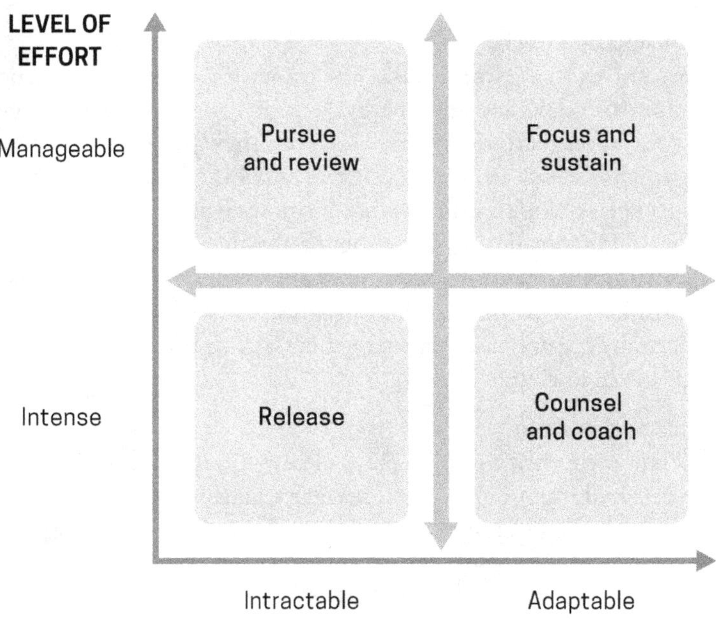

Figure 8.1: effort versus acceptance

Find the points of intersection to determine your best potential course of action:

1. **Release**
   If the level of effort required is intense, and their willingness to accept and adapt is almost nonexistent, then it's time to consider your options around their position. Is it time for them to trade this role for something else? Do they need to be moved to another role that has less leadership responsibility? If there are no internal options, do they need to look for options outside the organisation?
2. **Pursue and review**
   If the amount of time you need to spend is relatively low, but you are also seeing little progress, then it's time to check your willingness to put in more effort and their ability to shift. Will investing more time and effort change the situation, or are you just delaying the inevitable? Do they need a different type of support? What's holding them back from wanting or being able to change? Are there other strategies that need to be deployed to support their leadership development? What more do you expect of them, and are those expectations realistic?
3. **Counsel and coach**
   This can be tough. You feel like the leader is consuming enormous amounts of your time and energy, so much so that you aren't available for your other team members. However, they are trying to change, and you are seeing progress (albeit in small increments). I'd encourage you to keep going. Find out what more they need and what's holding them back. Consider if you've spent enough time coaching and supporting them and whether there are any mitigating circumstances that could have hampered their progress. As well, consider their understanding and acceptance of their lack of progress, and whether that's likely to change.
4. **Focus and sustain**
   This is a great position to be in, as clearly the work is paying off. The leader is making progress to close their leadership gaps and you are happy with the level of effort you are putting in. Keep going.

Take a moment and ask yourself, is enough enough?

It's decision time

Your next step may be to recognise that your direct report needs more time and you need to reassess the strategies you are using. If that's the case, go back to chapter 6, re-examine the strategies you decided to employ and see what else might be deployed. Also, encourage the leader to dig into Part III of this book and apply those learnings to their leadership development.

If you are considering demoting, moving someone or letting them go, you need to plan and manage these actions carefully. There are laws to protect employees (and rightly so). You have to ensure your assessment is fair and that you've given your direct report enough time to change their leadership style.

> This isn't the time for the Donald Trump approach to firing employees and colleagues!

Many years ago I had a team member who wasn't performing. It was complicated by the fact that she was also dating the company's Head of HR. I had people around me saying, 'You can't do anything about this. She's a protected species'. I couldn't ignore the problem, though, as it was impacting the rest of the team. I had to deal with it, and that meant having a very upfront conversation with the Head of HR, who was entirely professional about the situation. He knew she was struggling too, and he supported my decision.

You may worry about fallout. You may think it's too hard and seek an easier path. You may be overly emotionally invested because you really like the person. You may even worry because they are a top revenue performer and moving them on could impact your business results in the short to medium term. But as the author J.K. Rowling has said, 'It is our choices that show what we truly are, far more than our abilities.'

It's very easy to make head-based decisions. There are lots of tools out there to you help you do that. You can list the pros and cons, workshop the idea with trusted colleagues, explore the risk–reward trade-off and write a decision tree.

There are times when you also need to think with your heart. Heart-based decisions go beyond thinking with your head or relying on instinct. They challenge you to approach the decision differently by looking at the issue from multiple perspectives.

With a heart-based decision you ask yourself these questions:

- If I was courageous, what would I do?
- If I put the needs of others before my own, what would I do?
- If I examined this decision from an ethical perspective, would my decision change?
- If I took a compassionate approach, what would I do?
- Will I be proud to share my involvement in this decision with the people I most care about?

And remember, sometimes the kindest thing you can do is to help a person move on to another role where they can be their best.

This is not the time to go into avoidance mode by delaying the decision or trying to find a way to delegate it to someone else, usually HR.

This is not HR's role. It's your role.

This decision doesn't affect just you. It affects the leader, their team and other leaders in your team. You need to think long term.

Bad leadership is contagious. A toxic culture creates stress and mental health issues, undermines workplace effectiveness and generally makes everyone involved miserable. This isn't fun and the responsibility rests with you, because you have a duty of care to the people in your teams.

Good decision making is at the heart of successful organisations and is a hallmark of great leaders.

Lessons learned

If, after all, you find yourself in the position where you need to let the leader go, examine what you can take away from the experience.

TIME OUT

- Could you have acted sooner?
- Were there warning signs you missed?
- If you hired them, was there a failure or gap in the hiring process?
- What would you do differently next time?

As well, consider the impact this decision may have on your team and the leader's team. Check in to make sure they are okay. Manage any fallout or concerns. Make sure they feel supported through the process. A change of leader can be unsettling for people, even if they are happy to see the person go. You will also want to put in place support mechanisms to help the team as they manage the interim period with no leader and when they transition to a new leader.

On the other hand, if the leader is sticking around and you continue working with them, stay focused. Don't lose sight of the goal, and don't let them lose focus either. You want their new ways of leading to become fully and permanently embedded.

Your leadership legacy

Being a leader is a privilege, not a right. Each day you affect the people around you, and the choices you make will shape whether that impact elevates them or diminishes them. It's so easy as a leader to think that change starts with others, but it always starts with you — shifting, shaping and adapting. Doing more. Being more.

In the words of the Sufi poet Rumi: 'Yesterday I was clever, so I wanted to change the world. Today I am wise, so I am changing myself.'

On the field

In a conversation with me, Johan, a senior executive in the latter stages of his career, reflected on the highs and lows of his leadership journey. He said to me, 'Michelle, when I think back to the best times, it wasn't about what I achieved by myself, it was what we achieved together.'

His lowest points were the times when he, as the leader of leaders, wasn't at the top of his game, and he let his team down by not backing them or not being available enough.

His learnings? Take action earlier when things aren't working, spend more time with the team, and always think long term when it comes to developing the team.

Leadership is often so much easier in hindsight, which is why learning, stepping up and being ready to change as a leader (and leader of leaders) never stops.

PART III

What to do if you ... ARE ONE

You may have bought this book because you are working for a challenging boss and you think, 'I'm not a bad boss so I can skip this part. It doesn't relate to me.' Well, not so fast.

If you manage people, or even *one* person, then you are a boss (regardless of how you see yourself or how the organisation labels you), and you need to check that how you *think* you're managing or leading matches the reality of how you're *actually* managing or leading.

You may think you're nailing it, yet sadly the truth may be far from that.

Reading this part will help generate valuable insights into your behaviour and whether you're up to par. On the other hand, if you are reading this because your boss's actions are making your working life hell, then this section will also enhance your understanding and ability to work with them.

No normal person wakes up in the morning and thinks, 'My goal today is to be a totally crap boss and to make the working day for my team members hell.' Yet it frequently works out that way. Why?

As a boss or a leader, you may be:

- ill-equipped for the role
- working for a boss who puts unreasonable demands on you (Part I will also help you with this)
- hampered by a low level of self-awareness
- blind to the impact you're having on your team and colleagues
- struggling to handle the pressure
- working in a toxic environment
- oblivious to what good leadership is.

One of the best leaders I worked for during my corporate career challenged me on how I saw myself. I had just been promoted to a junior manager role and I was feeling pretty chuffed with myself. I'd worked hard, was getting results, being professional and doing what I thought a leader did — delegating, getting stuff done, setting the team's direction and managing the workflow in a calm, professional way.

I thought things were going well — until my boss drew me aside and said, 'You know, Michelle, I get that you're ambitious and that you want to do a good job. The work's important, but when you move on, no one will remember the work you did. The only thing they'll remember is how you made them *feel.'*

It was a great wake-up call. I started making changes, and found the more I connected with my team, the more I understood them and their needs, and vice versa. Our working relationship got better, we got more done as a team and were collectively more successful because I put them first.

Your tone and behaviour set the standard for what's acceptable and unacceptable in your team, so it's important you know the truth about your management and leadership!

Being a great leader takes work, but above all else it takes a desire to do better. The fact you've got this far shows you want that too.

9
ASSESS
WHERE YOU'RE AT

I was in Virgin's airport lounge in Sydney, Australia, waiting to catch a plane back to Melbourne, when Sir Richard Branson dropped by to say hello to guests and chat with staff. Apparently, he does that every time he is in town. No doubt he's busy, but he finds the time to do it because he knows that taking the time for people matters. It also has direct business benefits because it makes the employees feel good about working at Virgin, and it makes the customers feel appreciated and pleased they chose to fly Virgin. (I know I did.)

Now let me compare Richard Branson's actions with a CEO I used to work with. If this CEO walked past you in the corridor, he would actively avoid eye contact so he didn't have to interact with you. The message it sent was he wasn't interested and couldn't be bothered to make the effort.

> You need to find time for your people — they matter, and they deserve to be acknowledged and respected.

Christine Porath, an Associate Professor of Management at Georgetown University, found that respect tops the charts for employees. Her survey of 20 000 employees around the world, conducted in conjunction with *Harvard Business Review* and Tony Schwartz, concluded that being treated with respect was more important to employees than recognition and appreciation, having an inspiring vision, receiving feedback, or having opportunities for learning and development.

The research found that respected employees reported:

- 56 per cent better health and wellbeing
- 1.72 times more trust and safety
- 89 per cent more enjoyment and job satisfaction
- 92 per cent greater focus and prioritisation.

I mean, who wouldn't want to work for someone who:

- helps them be their best
- believes in them and their potential
- empowers them to act, and helps them succeed
- provides meaningful coaching and opportunities for growth
- demonstrates through words and actions that they matter
- provides the necessary support, feedback and resources so they can progress
- makes time for them?

Sadly, though, many bosses think they are doing a great job and are shocked when they discover their team think otherwise.

The best leaders proactively seek feedback and continually assess their effectiveness. Making time to assess your leadership doesn't automatically catapult you into a 'good boss' category. It does, however, make you someone who's interested and invested in being the best leader they can be.

Time to open your eyes

Most of us have an image of our ideal 'self'. We picture how we respond to certain situations, or what we might say or do if presented with a certain problem. We don't always live up to our expectations, however. Quite often we act in ways that are less than desirable, yet we can't quite explain why.

These are our blind spots, or what Swiss psychiatrist and psychoanalyst Carl Jung called in his 1951 book *Aion* our 'shadow self'. He explains: 'The shadow is a moral problem that challenges the whole ego-personality, for no one can become conscious of the shadow without considerable moral effort. To become conscious of it involves recognizing the dark aspects of the personality as present and real. This act is the essential condition for any kind of self-knowledge.'

The shadow is anything that is outside your awareness and consciousness. It comprises those aspects of your personality that you want to reject and suppress. Jung believed we distance ourselves from thoughts and ideas we don't like, rather than confront and deal with them.

The shadow isn't all dark, though; there is light too. The dark can include aggressive and immoral impulses, experiences of shame, irrational desires or unacceptable sexual fantasies, while the light is often hidden in people who hold self-limiting beliefs about themselves, experiencing low self-esteem and high anxiety.

As you deny these character traits in yourself, you recognise and dislike them in other people. You can also unfairly project these characteristics on other people.

For example, in the work environment you may be quick to judge others and point out their flaws and insecurities, or to blame and exert power over others. Denying these actions and projecting them onto others is a way of protecting yourself.

To be an effective leader you have to make the 'unconscious' self a 'conscious' self.

Hence, the first step to change is opening your eyes to what is really going on.

Pressure to perform

It's important to reflect critically and honestly on what is actually going on in your world and how you feel you are doing. What internal or external circumstances are affecting you?

The expectations on leaders and bosses these days are HUGE. You work long hours, are always on call, and must sort out complex problems and juggle competing demands, all the while knowing you face permanent job insecurity.

Throw in an overly demanding boss, or stakeholders who don't support and back you, or an unpleasant work environment, and the pressure rises to bursting point. (Remember the pressure chamber first discussed in the Introduction!)

Leading people can take its toll on your health.

Academics Ronald Heifetz and Marty Linsky, experts in building adaptive leaders, note that when things get busy and tough and the adrenaline is pumping, it's easy for leaders to convince themselves that they won't succumb to the normal human frailties, but the 'intellectual, physical and emotional challenges of leadership are fierce'. To manage, they recommend leaders 'regularly step into the inner chamber of your being and assess the tolls those challenges are taking'.

Pressure may come from your boss, your work colleagues, your team members or other sources. But the issue isn't about where the pressure comes from; it's about the frequency and strength of the pressure and your ability to cope with it.

When the pressure becomes too much, you'll find the 'go to' coping strategies you have successfully used before no longer work. Deep down you know you aren't being the best version of you, but you feel trapped and don't know the way out.

TIME OUT

- Do you wake up in the morning looking forward to work?
- Do you have a healthy and constructive relationship with your boss?
- Do you feel you're making progress at work on things that matter?
- Do you have enough resources and skills to do your job effectively?
- Do you rarely (if ever) have feelings of overwhelm and anxiety at work?
- Do you have healthy and engaged relationships at home and at work?
- Are you taking care of your mind, body and spirit through regular exercise and meditation, eating well and finding time for other self-care practices?

If in answering these questions you realise that much of the pressure is coming from your relationship with your boss, then I'd suggest you begin by going back and rereading Part I on how to better work for a bad (or perhaps just challenging) boss.

> You can't work on your own leadership until you've addressed what might be the real or contributory factors.

Living your leadership potential every day requires you to know and address any factors that may be negatively impacting you. But this doesn't mean you walk away from your responsibility. You also need to step up and challenge yourself about the part you are playing.

Green, yellow or red?

In some team sports, when a player violates the rules or behaviour codes they are shown a card by the referee. A yellow card is a warning to change their behaviour, while a red card indicates a more serious offence and usually results in the player being sent off the field immediately.

They don't use a green card in sports, but you will as you navigate this chapter to identify specific behaviours and determine if you are being your best.

Life is never clear cut. No doubt you'll act in certain ways sometimes, but in quite different ways at other times. You need to identify your dominant patterns, because it's those patterns that largely define how your leadership is assessed by those around you.

You'll do this by looking at seven key leadership indicators:

1. awareness
2. authenticity
3. mission
4. mindset
5. authority
6. relationship style
7. team norms.

For each indicator you will assess yourself, giving yourself a red, yellow or green card to identify any gaps requiring improvement.

Remember, a low score does not necessarily mean you are a 'bad' leader, manager or person. This is about being honest with yourself to see where you could be performing better and elevating your team's progress.

1. Awareness

Organisational psychologist Tasha Eurich has examined the concept of self-awareness—what it is and what it isn't, why we need it and how to increase it. She found that 95 per cent of us believe we're self-aware, even though only about 10 to 15 per cent of us actually are.

From her review of existing research, she distinguished two sides to self-awareness:

1. **Internal self-awareness**. How clearly do you notice and identify your values, passions, aspirations, fit with your environment, thoughts, feelings and behaviours, and the impact you have on others? Internal self-awareness is positively correlated with job and relationship satisfaction, personal and social control, and happiness; it's negatively associated with anxiety, stress and depression.
2. **External self-awareness**. How accurately do you understand how other people view you across the same factors listed for internal self-awareness? External self-awareness is positively correlated with empathy and perspective taking, and therefore a greater ability to build healthy and satisfying relationships.

Even when you feel you know yourself and what drives your thoughts and behaviours, there will be times when those motivations are interpreted differently by colleagues and team members. This is why both elements of self-awareness are crucial for effective leadership.

As a boss you need to be both internally and externally aware.

So let's check in on your first leadership indicator and assess your level of internal and external self-awareness.

Leadership Indicator 1: Leadership Awareness

Check the column that best represents your response.

DO YOU:	RED (RARELY)	YELLOW (SOMETIMES)	GREEN (USUALLY)
Spend time digging into your feelings, thought processes and behaviours to understand what motivates your actions?			
Notice when events or people at work trigger a 'fight or flight' response in you?			
Understand why you have been triggered?			
Reflect on the impact the working environment has on how you feel, think and act?			
Seek feedback on your leadership behaviours and practice?			
Know how people see you and describe you (that is, have a clear sense of your reputation and personal brand)?			
'For this indicator I am giving myself an overall .... card.'			

If you want additional help in determining your level of self-awareness, complete Tasha Eurich's online Insight Quiz.

2. Authenticity

Every time you make a decision you are on show: when you hire, fire or promote someone; when you dish out rewards, recognition and pay rises; when you give more attention to one team member than another; when you cancel a team meeting; the way you react when something goes wrong; when you take or share credit for success; when you fly business class and expect everyone else to fly economy; when you go home early or stay back late at work.

People will make assumptions about what you did, why you did it and who you are as a leader. You will be judged on your actions, intentions, values, integrity, trustworthiness and worth as a leader.

> It's really easy for there to be a disconnect between how you want to be seen (your promise) and how you are actually seen (your practice).

We all like to think of ourselves in a positive light. We hold this image of ourselves as a 'good person', using it as a reference point when we make decisions and constructing an internal dialogue to maintain it.

Yet our behaviour is influenced by two key factors that mean we may not be as 'good' as we think we are. These are:

1. espoused values versus values in use
2. moral licensing.

In 1974, Professors Chris Argyris and Donald Schön first drew a distinction between 'espoused values' and 'values in use'. Your espoused values are the values you talk about; your values in use are the values you live by in your daily life. For example, you might say you value honesty (your espoused value), yet when you receive honest criticism you become resentful (your values in use). You might say as a leader you encourage your team to ask questions (espoused values), yet criticise people who take up time asking questions (values in use).

This gap between the two sets of values can be evident in many aspects of life.

Your behavioural choices get even trickier when you discover that the act of doing something good, which boosts your image of yourself, can oddly give you permission to be not so good later. For example, you have had a highly productive morning so you decide to cruise through the afternoon; or you gave one team member very positive feedback, which you feel gives you licence to be harder on someone else later in the day.

In social psychology this is called 'moral licensing'.

It's a series of checks and balances.

Your brain holds an image of yourself and wants to maintain that image, so it keeps score of 'good' and 'bad' behaviours. You earn credits for good behaviours and debits for not so good behaviours, with the eventual aim of balancing the scales.

Researchers at Northwestern University ran a series of experiments to demonstrate this in practice. They found that 'priming people with positive and negative traits strongly affected moral behaviour'. This led people to behave either less morally (in the case of positive traits) or more morally (in the case of negative traits).

Often this happens subconsciously, and because we have a strong urge to maintain a positive image of ourselves we rewrite the narrative that accompanies behaviour that isn't congruent with who we think we are (or want to be).

All this means you need to be constantly alert to the signals, whether weak or strong, as to your behaviour and its congruence with your stated values and leadership vision.

One of the most effective ways of identifying the gap between your promise and practice is to source detailed and honest feedback.

During my corporate career, I participated in a number of 360-degree feedback processes. Every assessment tool helped me understand myself a little better. Sometimes the feedback was easy to take, other times not so easy. I learned that I needed to take an open heart and a curious mind into the process. I had to respect the opinions presented and look for the opportunities for growth.

Seek feedback from peers, colleagues, your team members and your boss, then check in to ask yourself, how authentically am I leading?

Leadership Indicator 2: Leadership Authenticity

Check the column that best represents your response.

DO YOU:	RED (RARELY)	YELLOW (SOMETIMES)	GREEN (USUALLY)
Have a leadership vision and values that are clear, transparent and lived?			
Exhibit consistent and reliable behaviours regardless of who is in the room?			
Hold firm to your moral compass and values regardless of the work environment?			
Have little to no gap between your stated values/leadership promise and your lived values/ leadership practice?			
Own your behaviour, always acting with integrity?			
Own your mistakes, taking full accountability?			
'For this indicator I am giving myself an overall .... card.'			

3. Mission

The concept of servant leadership has been around for centuries, but it was Robert Greenleaf's 1970 essay 'The Servant as Leader' that brought it to the surface.

A servant leader starts with a desire to serve. They focus on the growth and wellbeing of people and their community, while sharing power and putting the needs of others first. They are clear on who they are serving, making it is easier to focus on what matters, build the team and secure the desired outcomes.

Greenleaf wrote, 'The difference manifests itself in the care taken by the servant—first to make sure that other people's highest priority needs are being served. The best test ...: Do those served grow as persons? Do they, while being served, become healthier, wiser, freer, more autonomous, more likely themselves to become servants?'

Researchers from the University of Johannesburg examined existing research and found eight defining characteristics of this leadership style:

1. authenticity
2. humility
3. compassion
4. accountability
5. courage
6. altruism
7. integrity
8. listening.

Some of these characteristics challenge prevailing stereotypes of what it means to lead—particularly humility and altruism. (Ever seen those in a job description?)

Writing about how to identify the early warning signs of success or failure by looking at the CEO's behaviour, Tim Laseter from Strategy& (PwC) highlights the importance of humility, which he suggests is more prevalent among veteran executives than we might think. This is because those CEOs know that it operates as a 'powerful counterpoint to narcissism and dismissiveness. Indeed, it takes great self-confidence *not* to use power and influence to force compliance, and to humbly expose one's opinions to open debate.'

The Johannesburg researchers also found that a servant leadership approach is positively correlated with employee engagement, innovative behaviour, organisational commitment, trust, self-efficacy, job satisfaction and work–life balance, while it is negatively correlated with burnout and an employee's intention to leave an organisation. It also led to positive team dynamics including team identification and culture, and helped to improve customer service and sales.

Sadly, often leaders put their own needs first. This 'me first' approach does little to create strong team dynamics and an environment in which everyone excels.

A 'me first' approach doesn't inspire or motivate team members to be their best.

The best leaders know that for success they must consider the 'we', not just the 'me'. They know it's not just about them; it's about the team and what the team needs. So how do you score?

Leadership Indicator 3: Leadership Mission

Check the column that best represents your response.

DO YOU:	**RED (RARELY)**	**YELLOW (SOMETIMES)**	**GREEN (USUALLY)**
Put others first, thinking about their needs, not just your own?			
Share the credit and rewards, being humble and generous?			
Ensure your team members feel valued, respected and recognised?			
Focus on building and developing your team?			
Proactively approach your team to offer support and ask what they need from you?			
Ensure your team members are set up for success?			
Seek to elevate people around you?			

Never get your team members to do things you yourself wouldn't be prepared to do?			
Not waste your team's time, ensuring you don't ask for things you don't need?			
'For this indicator I am giving myself an overall .... card.'			

4. Mindset

At work you'll come across two types of leaders — those who approach leading with an abundance mentality and those who approach it with a scarcity mentality.

A feast or famine mindset impacts how you connect and lead.

In a highly competitive work environment, leaders can often act as though there aren't enough resources, rewards or recognition (the 3 Rs) to go around. Operating with this famine mindset means they jealously guard access to the 3 Rs, seeing them as crucial to career success.

A leader with this famine mindset worries that if someone else gets the same amount or more than they do it will diminish them. This has huge implications for how they work, as they approach conversations and negotiations with the objective of getting as much as they can for themselves. They are also less willing to collaborate and think about other people's needs, and struggle to admit mistakes.

Jon Maner, Professor of Management and Organisations at the Kellogg School of Management, also found that leaders who feel insecure about their position can intentionally sideline high-performing team members and inhibit communication and social bonding across the team in order to shore up their position.

By contrast, a leader with a feast mindset sees the work environment as full of opportunity, with more than enough to go around. They look to expand relationships and to collaborate with the goal of securing joint outcomes.

In doing this, they reframe the discussion from 'I must win at all costs' to 'How do we both walk away satisfied?' By doing this they take a long-term view of relationships, recognise and respect people's different needs, and understand that when someone else gets what they need it doesn't mean they will lose out.

What do you do?

Leadership Indicator 4: Leadership Mindset

Check the column that best represents your response.

DO YOU:	**RED (RARELY)**	**YELLOW (SOMETIMES)**	**GREEN (USUALLY)**
Share resources and ideas, knowing it will lead to better shared outcomes?			
Welcome the success and ideas of others?			
Feel secure about your abilities and employability?			
Promote the skills and successes of your team members?			
Provide positive feedback and recognition across the team?			
Cooperate for the general good, not just your own gain?			
Act ethically, always, in your dealings with others?			
Seek to 'collaborate and thrive', rather than 'divide and conquer'?			

Have clear and open ways of working, rather than hidden agendas?			
Enter a negotiation or discussion thinking how to best balance everyone's needs to get a fair outcome?			
'For this indicator I am giving myself an overall .... card.'			

5. Authority

Abraham Lincoln said, 'Nearly all men can stand adversity, but if you want to test a man's character, give him power.'

In his book *The Power Paradox*, Dacher Keltner, a Professor of Psychology at the University of California, writes that power is something we acquire by improving the lives of other people in our social network. In this way, power is granted to us by others. However, he notes, often our very experience of power destroys the skills that gave us the power in the first place. His research indicates that people who feel powerful are more likely to act impulsively—for example, to have affairs, drive aggressively, communicate in rude or disrespectful ways, or be dishonest.

In one of his experiments, dubbed 'The Cookie Monster Study', he divided participants into groups of three and randomly chose one in each group to be the leader. They were given a relatively menial writing task to complete, and half an hour into the task a plate of four cookies was brought in. Everyone took one cookie, but all group members initially left one cookie on the plate, because they didn't want to be *that* person who was so rude and greedy as to take the last cookie.

But that didn't stop the cookie monster eventually appearing, and invariably it was the person randomly chosen to be the leader who took the last cookie. This person, who felt more powerful, was also more likely to eat with their mouth open, lips smacking and scattering crumbs.

Dacher observed, 'If you give people power, they kind of look like brain trauma patients' in terms of how they behave. Subsequently, by behaving in this way, they lose the power that was bestowed on them in the first place.

Studies have also revealed that people in positions of power are three times more likely than other employees to interrupt colleagues, raise their voice and insult others. A 2010 study by the University of Southern California and London Business School, 'Power and overconfident decision-making', found a correlation between overconfidence and how much power a person has.

The more powerful a person feels, the more confident they are of the accuracy of their thoughts and beliefs. This means people in powerful positions are more confident that their opinions are correct, which may result in their failing to heed advice, ask questions or look for alternative opinions—all of which can hamper effective decision making.

When you start to think you're the smartest person in the room, you need to find another room.

What are the warning signs you may be drunk on power?

Leadership Indicator 5: Leadership Authority

Check the column that best represents your response.

DO YOU:	**RED (RARELY)**	**YELLOW (SOMETIMES)**	**GREEN (USUALLY)**
Create collective power and seek to share it for the benefit of all, rather than using power as a weapon for personal gain?			
Manage the political game, as opposed to playing the political game?			
Share control and empower your team, rather than micro-managing?			

Use and share information to make better decisions?			
Have open and constructive debates with your team members in which they can challenge your opinions?			
Listen to other people, recognising you don't have all the answers?			
Consider all perspectives and recognise you don't hold an exclusive licence on being right?			
'For this indicator I am giving myself an overall .... card.'			

6. Relationship style

New Zealand's Prime Minister, Jacinda Ardern, is revered for her compassion, authenticity and relevance. Since becoming prime minister in 2017, she has exceeded the expectations of many, with people across the globe praising her leadership style as both refreshingly different and desperately needed.

In the aftermath of the March 2019 terrorist attack on two local Christchurch mosques, Ardern was quick to condemn the violence. Wearing a headscarf out of respect for the Muslim community, she spoke quietly with and hugged the mourners, her shock and compassion clearly unfeigned. Speaking in Parliament after the attack she said of this community in mourning, 'Let us acknowledge their grief as they do. Let's support them as they gather again for worship. We are one, they are us.' She ended her speech with the words 'Tatau tatau. [Everyone.] Al salam Alaikum. Weh Rahmat Allah. Weh Barakaatuh. [May peace and mercy and God's blessings be upon you.]'

Inevitably there were some who denounced her for wearing a headscarf, just as others criticised her strong stance on climate change and decisions she has made affecting New Zealand's economy.

Leadership isn't a popularity contest.

There will always be someone ready to criticise and condemn you, but part of being a leader is taking a stand on things that matter.

Having worked across many industry sectors and functional disciplines from junior to senior levels, I acknowledge that leadership isn't easy. You have choices to make every day in how you lead and learn. These choices contribute to creating either a culture of denial and exclusion, or an environment of opportunity and inclusion — for you, your team and your colleagues.

It's about stepping up, finding your unique style, building constructive relationships, making the tough decisions and being courageous.

Many years ago I worked for a person who didn't like disappointing people by saying 'no', so he would say 'yes' perhaps too often. The problem was he was saying 'yes' to other people in the team, knowing it would lead to conflicting outcomes.

For example, I'd be working on a project and ask for approval, and unknown to me one of my peers would be working on something that conflicted with what I was doing. Both of us were given a 'yes', even though our work conflicted. We would both stumble across this problem later, then be left to find a way through the confusion. When we approached our manager with the issue his response was, 'I knew you two would sort it out eventually'!

He didn't want to be seen as the 'bad guy', the naysayer, so he would take the easy way out. He would either sugar-coat the message or say nothing at all.

Being a leader is harder when you are striving to please everyone and be everyone's favourite.

As Pulitzer Prize–winning journalist Herbert Swope put it, 'I cannot give you the formula for success, but I can give you the formula for failure, which is: Try to please everybody.'

Dr Brené Brown advises, 'Clear is kind. Unclear is unkind.' The power of that advice is in its simplicity. Think about it. When you give unclear instructions about what you want done, when you aren't willing to step into the tough conversations, when you aren't willing to give feedback — you aren't being kind.

You are giving yourself the easy option. You aren't spending time with your team members outlining your expectations, and you are stepping away from the conversations you need to have.

A failure to talk about the hard stuff invariably creates an environment of stunted opportunity, slow progress and toxic behaviour. This is because the problems go underground, festering and eventually blowing up, bigger and more troublesome than if you'd stepped in earlier.

By avoiding the conversation, you also miss the opportunity to deepen and strengthen your relationships. Employees want feedback—genuine feedback—and it's your responsibility to provide it.

Having real conversations is at the heart of real relationships.

What are the warning signs you are stepping away from the tough decisions and courageous conversations?

Leadership Indicator 6: Relationship Style

Check the column that best represents your response.

DO YOU:	**RED (RARELY)**	**YELLOW (SOMETIMES)**	**GREEN (USUALLY)**
Step into the tough conversations?			
Know your values, and willingly back them even if this means personal sacrifice or challenging perspectives of people senior to you?			
Focus on getting the best outcome rather than just pleasing people?			
ARE YOU:			
A builder of deep relationships and strong, compassionate networks, rather than being cynical, aloof and hard to get to know, creating shallow and transactional relationships?			

'For this indicator I am giving myself an overall .... card.'

7. Team norms

A recent opinion piece in *The New York Times* discussed the issue of extreme overwork. Among a broad range of examples of the unhealthy culture of long working hours, Jack Ma, Alibaba's founder and China's richest man, praised the 'blessing' of China's '996 practice' (which sees people working 9 am to 9 pm six days a week), while Uber's mantra was once 'Work smarter, harder and longer'.

Long hours are one cause of stress. In your organisation, the main contributing factor may be unreasonable demands, relentless churn and change, a lack of appreciation or inadequate resourcing. Whatever the source (or sources), when your team is stressed you won't be getting the best from them. They'll be less productive, more prone to burnout, more likely to exhibit dysfunctional behaviours and less able to solve complex problems.

In 2012, Google started a research project, code-named Project Aristotle, to figure out what made the best teams. Initially, they thought it would be about the smarts of the people in the team, but over time they came to realise it had far more to do with heart.

A year into the five-year study, they realised that having clear group norms was fundamental. The next step was to figure out what team norms mattered the most. Further study and research concluded that at the core was the need for psychological safety, a term coined by Harvard Professor Amy Edmondson.

'Psychological safety,' she suggested, 'isn't about being nice. It's about giving candid feedback, openly admitting mistakes, and learning from each other.' It's also about knowing your team won't embarrass, reject or punish you. The team trust and respect one another, so you can come to work and be your authentic self.

I first read about Google's research in a 2016 article by Charles Duhigg in *The New York Times* titled 'What Google learned from its quest to build the perfect team'. Duhigg wrote, 'No one wants to put on a "work face" when they get to the office. No one wants to leave part of their personality and inner life at home.' To be able to talk openly, though, we need to feel safe.

> Setting team norms and creating an environment in which each team member can be their best self requires deliberate thought and action.

What are you doing to create the most effective team norms?

Leadership Indicator 7: Team Norms

Check the column that best represents your response.

DO YOU:	RED (RARELY)	YELLOW (SOMETIMES)	GREEN (USUALLY)
Establish practices to create psychological safety in your team?			
Spend time discussing and agreeing on the team's norms and ways of working?			
Have a clear team purpose that connects the team and how they work together?			
Deal quickly with any problematic behaviours that could impact team members and how they work together?			
Listen first and clarify, ensuring equal airtime, rather than dominating conversations?			
Use constructive emotions and actions to promote the right team dynamics?			
Have realistic expectations about what your team members can achieve?			
Have appropriate downtime and support so your team are managing their workloads well?			
Have an agreed way of dealing with work required outside of standard business hours?			

Make it easy for your employees to come to you with requests or questions?			
Encourage your team to switch off?			
Make time to troubleshoot problems with your team?			
Spend an appropriate amount of time in your working week with your team?			
Seek to raise your team members up to their highest level?			
'For this indicator I am giving myself an overall .... card.'			

How did you score?

The purpose of that exercise is to get an indication of your leadership gaps and where you should focus your attention, not to berate yourself or to pat yourself on the back. As with any self-rating system, you may have been too harsh or too kind to yourself.

Take a moment to review all seven indicators to see where you landed. In which areas did you do well, and what needs improving? Did any results surprise you?

In the next chapter, we will take your new insights and learnings, and strategise ways to close the gaps and move your rankings to green across all areas.

On the field

Antony was used to being seen as the superstar. He'd done well and progressed up through the ranks quickly. He was an expert in his technical field, and after a promotion he inherited an established, well-respected team.

But then he stalled.

Antony's leadership style was underdeveloped and consequently the team struggled to work well with him, losing focus and momentum. This was noticed by Antony's leader, who helped him work through the gap between his perception and the reality of his leadership style.

He told me how this wasn't easy to hear and he initially challenged it, but he took the time to assess, and with greater awareness came acceptance.

As with all change, this wasn't an overnight success story. You can't expect instantaneous results. It requires commitment, focus and a strong desire to improve.

10 STRATEGISE YOUR DEVELOPMENT

In his book *Commander in Cheat: How Golf Explains Trump,* former *Sports Illustrated* columnist Rick Reilly analyses Donald Trump's behaviour on the golf course as a way of explaining his ethics, modus operandi and leadership style.

Trump loves to play golf. He owns 14 courses around the world and operates another five. He boasts they are the 'best on the planet', that he has a handicap of 3 (which is excellent), rarely loses and has won 18 club championships.

In his research Reilly was unable to substantiate any of the club championships. He explains how Trump cheats, sometimes with the help of his caddies and Secret Service agents, by getting them to move his badly hit golf balls to better positions. He also lies about his golfing scores (what Reilly has titled the 'Trump Bump') and ignores the game's rules of etiquette. At the same time, he inflates the worth of the golf courses he owns, happily underpays contractors and ignores the concerns of neighbours who live near his golf courses.

As with every aspect of his life, for Trump it's about winning. Never admitting defeat. Never admitting he is wrong. Putting himself first and using all the tricks in the book to beat his way to the top. That's his strategy.

On the surface you could say it's working. He often does get his own way, but it's not a sustainable strategy over the long term. It's certainly not a strategy to deploy if you want happy, healthy, engaged and motivated employees!

Trump has set a record staff turnover rate within his Administration. Kathryn Dunn Tenpas, a Senior Fellow at the Brookings Institution, has tracked turnover at all levels of what is dubbed 'the A team' at a whopping 77 per cent as at 10 September 2019. This includes critical roles such as the US National Security Advisor, the President's Press Secretary and his Chief of Staff.

When you are a bad boss you negatively impact productivity and engagement levels, which increases turnover and can mean you struggle to recruit the right calibre of staff to your team.

If your reputation for being a bad boss is well known, you'll find it harder to get promoted and to maintain employment.

But more than that, wouldn't you rather work in and facilitate an environment where you are at your best, and so too are your team members?

Nothing beats being in a team where people thrive and the work hums. This doesn't mean you're working on stuff that's easy. Quite the contrary. I often found the best teams and the best boss when I was working on projects that were hard, challenging and complex. My boss and co-workers had my back. I had theirs. My strengths were being used. The work was interesting. It was awesome.

As a leader, you are faced with a choice. Either you can do little or nothing about your identified leadership gaps, which means your leadership doesn't improve and nothing changes in your team environment; or you can take serious action to address your leadership gaps, then over time see your leadership improve and your team environment thrive.

It's your call.

As written by others before: 'If your actions inspire others to dream more, learn more, do more and become more, you are a leader.'

Given you've got this far in the book, I suggest you not only want to *do* more, but you want to *be* more. Agreed?

Creating your leadership playbook

Every person is unique, which means every leader is unique. The action you need to take to elevate your leadership is different from what other people around you may need to do. This is about creating your own personal playbook filled with strategies and tactics that put you in the best possible position to lead with integrity, authenticity and courage.

To do this, we're going to return to the leading indicators identified in the previous chapter. Read through all the content here, paying particular attention to the indicators where you gave yourself a red or yellow card. Remember, it does not mean that you do these things 'badly'; rather, that you need to do them 'better'.

Indicator 1: Open your heart and mind to awareness

Being self-aware is a lifelong process and is certainly not a tick-the-box exercise. It requires a commitment to know yourself and understand your trigger points, a willingness to know what lurks in the shadows and why, an openness to feedback, and a strong desire to bring your best and whole self to work every day.

During my corporate career, working with the support of an executive coach, I learned to perceive how my behaviour was interpreted by others, and how my shadow side, which needed recognition and validation, drove my actions. I recognised and accepted I needed to show up in a different way. Because I was seen as impenetrable, I learned to share more of myself. I dropped my tendency towards perfectionism and driving things too hard, creating space for my team to explore and excel. None of this was a one-off activity; it needed constant effort—working with that coach, seeking feedback, meditating and reflecting.

You can make progress on your own too. It's helpful to reflect each day on who you are, what you've done and the outcomes. But be mindful that your brain is a master of reinvention and storytelling. It's easy to tell yourself a story about what something means when in fact it doesn't mean that at all.

Listen and learn

One of my clients had a major dilemma. He liked his boss but there were challenges, as they didn't always see eye to eye, and he was a bit temperamental, although it was manageable.

Until one day ... as part of the end-of-year performance review process each team member was asked to provide 360-degree feedback on the boss. My client provided the feedback assuming the input would be treated confidentially. It wasn't, and his boss, not liking what he read in the report, then made it his mission to discover who had given the negative feedback.

Once he had nailed that, the relationship between my client and his boss went downhill quickly. The boss started to sideline him, give him negative feedback and pretty much seize every opportunity to make his working day miserable. Eventually, HR had to intervene, making it all very unpleasant.

You can't learn and grow if you aren't open to hearing what you don't want to hear. True, not all feedback you receive will be useful, but you have to be open to it, understanding where it is coming from and then discerning what's helpful and what's not.

> The best leaders learn constantly, always seeking — in fact craving — feedback.

TIME OUT

- What feedback sources currently exist or need to be established for you to get regular and reliable feedback?

Indicator 2: Close the authenticity gap

Good leadership doesn't happen by accident. Sure, some people gravitate to leadership roles and are more naturally gifted at it, but the best leaders know leadership takes practice.

You have to strive to be the best you can be, recognising there will be hiccups along the way. It's hard to do that if you don't have clear intentions about what you want to be or do.

Writing your leadership manifesto will help. It will set out who you are, what you stand for and how you want to develop authentically as a leader.

There are four steps to this process:

1. Reflect on the current status
2. Shape your future
3. Get feedback
4. Live your manifesto

Let's look at each in turn.

Step 1: Reflect on the current status

In the previous chapter, you uncovered the gap between who you think you are as a leader (your leadership promise) and how your team experience you (your leadership practice).

Just as hoarders need to clean out their closets and throw away junk that is cluttering their home, you need to clean out your thoughts and throw away any beliefs, ideas and preconceived notions that are unhelpfully cluttering your leadership mind.

This takes insight, courage and a willingness to get uncomfortable.

> Often the biggest battle is the one you have within you.

It's looking at the unwritten rules of leadership you have been told to follow that don't serve your team and stop you being your best. It's identifying the limiting beliefs that are holding you back, or the ingrained patterns of behaving that need to shift. It's the stories you tell yourself about who you are as a leader.

Herminia Ibarra, the Charles Handy Professor of Organisational Behaviour at London Business School, has researched what can hold people, particularly leaders, back as they progress through their career. She found that our sense of who we are is shaped by our experiences and the meaning we put on those experiences in terms of the stories we tell ourselves. At certain points in our career, those stories are no longer helpful, and we need to find a new narrative.

'Most of us,' she writes, 'have personal narratives about defining moments that taught us important lessons. Consciously or not, we allow our stories, and the images of ourselves that they paint, to guide us in new situations.' She suggests that these stories can become outdated, and there may come a time when we need to revise or even replace them.

For you, that time is now. You already know there are gaps in your leadership and consequently that your leadership story needs to change.

To grow into a leader, you need to ditch any outdated beliefs, rules, assumptions and practices.

TIME OUT

- What are the expectations or unwritten rules that shape how you feel, think and lead?
- Do these expectations and rules help or hinder your leadership?
- What would you need to do to stop adhering to these rules?
- How would those changes elevate your leadership practice?

Step 2: Shape your future

It's now time to shape your future leadership vision. This is the 'where you want to get to' piece of the puzzle. Consider the leader you want to be, by asking yourself:

- What type of leader do you want to become?
- If you had to brand your desired leadership style using one word, what would it be?
- Where and how do you want to leave your mark in this world?
- How do you want the people you work with to feel and talk about you?
- What do you want to be known for?

Reflecting on your answers, use those insights to craft your leadership manifesto. These words set the standard for who you want to be, what you want to be remembered for and the defining characteristics of your leadership.

Step 3: Get feedback

Once you've spent time crafting and refining your leadership manifesto, the next step is to share it with a couple of trusted colleagues and friends. Get feedback from them and find out how it made them think and feel. Use that feedback to review and refine it.

Ask them:

- Was it inspirational, aspirational and authentically you?
- Did it resonate with them?
- Was it clear, concise and honest?
- Did it help them better understand your leadership journey—where you are now, and where you'd like to get to?

Step 4: Live your manifesto

As part of your leadership experience, it's really powerful to share your manifesto with your team. It will help them understand you, who you are, where you come from and what matters to you. I've seen leaders do this and it's a compelling way to build connection and trust across the team.

It's then your responsibility to bring that vision to life, hold it close to your heart, and notice when you are being authentic to your vision and when you are stepping away from it.

> Use your manifesto to reflect on and remind yourself about the leader and, ultimately, the person you want to be.

Indicator 3: Accept your mission

If you've seen or read Shakespeare's *Henry V* you'll know it's set before and after the famous Battle of Agincourt in 1415. The English troops were vastly outnumbered by the French, so victory looked uncertain. The night before the battle the King wandered around the English camp in disguise to gauge the soldiers' morale and lift their spirits. The next morning, Henry led his troops into battle and victory—from the front, as was his habit.

When I watched a theatre production of this play recently, I thought about how most of today's leaders lead, not from the front lines like Henry, but remotely, from isolated offices, passing down decrees via emails, SMS or social media.

The best leaders are those who are willing to get amongst it. Those who understand what it is like to be on the front line serving customers or working on the shopfloor. They are eager to experience the challenges staff confront so they are better informed and therefore able to make wiser decisions.

Leading from the front can't be done from the comfort of the corner office (or even your open-plan desk).

It's being willing to roll up your sleeves and actively engage with staff at all levels of the organisation so you really understand their frustrations and opportunities. It's actively leading the changes you are seeking to make by being the first to immerse yourself in those challenges. It's not expecting one rule for you, and a different set of rules for others. It's not asking your team members to do things you wouldn't be prepared to do. It's being approachable and willing to listen to ideas from people across the organisation. It's seeking ways to better understand your team members and their work so you can best support, develop and enhance their contribution.

It takes courage to step out in front. It can feel much safer and less risky to remain detached from the action. But stepping out in front is not about you. It's about the people you serve.

Remember the concept of servant leadership from the previous chapter? It's a people first approach, based on the idea that if you demonstrate a deep understanding of the needs of your team members, they will in turn engage more in their work and be more motivated to achieve their goals.

Sen Sendjaya, Professor of Leadership at Melbourne's Swinburne University of Technology, defines servant leadership as 'a holistic approach to leading that engages the rational, relational, emotional, ethical, and spiritual dimensions of the followers such that they are transformed into what they are capable of becoming'.

In looking at your work environment, what difference will it make to your team if you flip how you currently lead, so you prioritise your team members' needs over yours and you put your people first, rather than the task?

TIME OUT

- If you opt to put the 'we' before the 'me', how would you lead differently?
- How would this change how you make decisions, share information, communicate, delegate work, and give and receive feedback?
- How would you consult and engage with your team to ensure you best support their needs?

Your answers become key elements of your 'people first' strategy.

Now, you could easily lock yourself away and complete this exercise in isolation. Working alone, though, doesn't usually produce the best results—particularly when your objective is to elevate your leadership.

Talk with your team. What ideas do they have? What have they seen work in the past? Would your suggested actions address their collective and individual needs?

Indicator 4: Develop a feast mindset

Using your new operating philosophy of 'people first' requires a shift of mindset from famine to feast. It's leading from a place of care, compassion and humility.

When you are humble, you show your team you care. You don't put yourself first, hoarding all the glory and rewards. You consider the needs of others and seek to do the right thing for all concerned, whether team members, colleagues, stakeholders or customers. You create an environment that is safe and supportive, proactively seeking opportunities to promote and elevate your team members.

It's easy to characterise a caring organisational culture as one that is too soft and easy, failing to focus on profitable and sustainable outcomes. It's actually quite the contrary. When employees know they are cared for, they in turn are more likely to genuinely care about the customer and seek to ensure they receive the service or product that meets their needs. When customers are happy, the organisation's growth follows.

Mindset shifts are hard work and require deliberate practice where you regularly challenge your approach to situations. It's useful to have strategies in place to help you do this. This starts with developing your mindset-shifting process.

Shifting your mindset involves a four-part strategy:

1. **Listen to yourself**—and discover what you are feeling, thinking and saying about the situation or event.
2. **Recognise that you have a choice**—to approach it with a famine mindset or a feast mindset.
3. **Challenge your approach**—the way you are feeling and thinking—and determine the likely impact this approach will have on you and your team.
4. **Take action**—approaching the situation in a way that best aligns with your leadership vision and who you want to be.

Think about the mindset you typically adopt when challenged and identify your options to change so it better aligns with your new leadership approach.

Indicator 5: Break your power addiction

It's easy to feel like you hold all the power as the leader, but today that old authoritative leadership style needs to be not just temporarily unplugged but permanently disconnected!

Leadership is a privilege. Your position enables you to make decisions that can impact the lives of people around you—either for good or for not so good.

When you share power, your team are more willing to speak up and debate ideas, enabling good ideas to surface and bad ideas to be improved on.

It also encourages people to be themselves, and when your team members are themselves they will bring their best selves to work. This helps you, as the leader, to make better decisions because you know you no longer need to act as though you have all the answers. Instead your role is to facilitate interaction, encourage curiosity and support spirited conversations.

Research by Katherine Phillips, Associate Professor of Management and Organisations at the Kellogg School of Management, and colleagues found the more alike people are, the more likely they are to think along the same lines; therefore there is less room for debate, discernment and disagreement. Diverse groups outperform more homogeneous groups not because of an influx of new ideas, but because the diversity triggers more careful processing of the information discussed.

This approach helps to generate spirited conversations, rather than stilted, shallow, unproductive conversations. Spirited conversations create energy, spark new ideas, help people think about the position they hold, and encourage acceptance of different perspectives. It's embracing the power of questions.

The French anthropologist Claude Lévi-Strauss once said, 'The wise man doesn't give the right answers, he poses the right questions.'

Take a moment to consider other ways of sharing power across your team.

TIME OUT

- What opportunities are there to share power across the team?
- Which meetings involving senior stakeholders can you delegate?
- Which working group meetings can you get your team members involved in?
- How can decision making be altered to better facilitate collaboration and input?
- How can you communicate and share information across the team more effectively?

Indicator 6: Build courageous and healthy relationships

In 409 BC the Greek playwright Sophocles wrote his tragedy *Philoctetes*, set during the Trojan War, in which the protagonist Neoptolemus faces an ethical dilemma.

In a nutshell, Philoctetes is a great soldier who owns the bow and arrows of Hercules, which are needed for the Greeks to win the war, but the hero has been abandoned on an island in the middle of nowhere and bitten by a snake. Two soldiers, Odysseus and Neoptolemus, are sent to convince Philoctetes to come to Troy to join the battle. But Philoctetes is pretty pissed off. His snake wound is festering, and he doesn't like the Greeks.

Odysseus's solution is to get Neoptolemus to try to deceive Philoctetes into agreeing to come with them and fight the battle. But this idea doesn't go down well with Neoptolemus because he thinks it's dodgy and underhanded. He eventually agrees to the ruse, however, when he's convinced it's the only way to end the war with Troy. So Neoptolemus lies and tells a fanciful tale to Philoctetes to try to win him over. But eventually his principles catch up with him, and he admits to Philoctetes what he's done, and they become friends.

The moral of the story turns on the age-old debate around whether or when the ends justify the means. Is Neoptolemus justified in deceiving one man if he believes it's for the greater good (winning the war)? Odysseus's answer was 'yes', while Neoptolemus would rather fail with honour than win by cheating.

What about you? What position would you take in this kind of scenario, and what impact might that have on your reputation and how you build relationships?

I've seen leaders who, in an effort to be universally liked or to build a support base, gave up their voice, adjusted their views to conform with the people who had power, and lost sight of what they stood for. In doing this, they closed off aspects of who they were, suppressing their authentic self.

This does enormous damage to your confidence and sense of self-worth. Research from Kellogg University shows that when a person stops being their authentic self it causes psychological distress that can have ongoing emotional and physical ramifications. It also affects how people perceive and relate to you.

When people no longer know what you stand for, they start to question the intent of your actions, making it harder for them to collaborate with you and support the work you do.

Over time, this puts your career on the downhill slide, because you can't be successful without working effectively with colleagues, peers and team members.

By contrast, when you're authentic and stand behind your values, have a clear personal brand and behave consistently, it is far easier for team members and colleagues to connect with and trust you. They know that the person they see is the person you are, and that you won't let them down by saying one thing and doing another.

Think about the relationships you have at work—with colleagues or direct reports—and where you need to strengthen them.

Central to building real relationships is being ready and willing to have courageous conversations, where with your leadership vision clear you are being true to yourself and those around you.

TIME OUT

- Where are you stepping away from building diverse and authentic relationships?
- In what ways can you build deeper and more meaningful relationships?
- What conversations have you been putting off having, and what would be the benefit of having those conversations?

Indicator 7: Establish team norms and purpose

The story is told that when President John F. Kennedy was visiting NASA headquarters before the first moon landing he met a janitor who was mopping the floor. The President asked him what he did at NASA. His response: 'I'm helping put a man on the moon.'

Many would see this man's job as mundane and unimportant, but he had purpose. That purpose gave him focus, and no doubt a sense of fulfilment.

Often leaders use a 'them' and 'us' approach to binding the team together. However, this can be dangerous and create disconnection. I've seen leaders at town hall meetings speak disparagingly of their competitors, hoping it will inspire greater efforts from the team; instead, the leader just comes off looking mean-spirited and petty, which does nothing to build team spirit and solidarity.

Essentially teams are brought together to get things done. The logic is that people get more done together than alone. That benefit, however, is only achieved when the team has a common purpose and clarity on how they work together, and that doesn't always exist.

The leader will usually know what each team member is doing, and how each individual contributes to the whole. Sadly, often team members don't share the same level of understanding, which can cause frustration and friction.

Sometimes this can be because two teams have recently been merged, so the newly combined team's purpose and the role each team member needs to play isn't yet clear. Whatever the reason, this ambiguity breeds disengagement and distrust across the team, which negatively impacts how the team views your leadership effectiveness.

> Effective leaders know it's critical to get the team working together to achieve a joint outcome as quickly as possible, so the team makes progress on the right things at the right time.

Clarity of purpose also helps the team sustain focus when roadblocks appear and progress becomes challenging. So it's important to spend time with your team developing this shared purpose and discussing how you can best jointly bring it to life.

There are a number of ways you can do this. One effective method is to create a vision board, which captures the essence of your team's purpose—what you do, why you do it and where you want to get to as a team. It's visual and colourful, with images and words that help spark energy, emotion and connection.

Developing your team's vision board is also fun and an awesome way to get the creative juices flowing. Pull out the coloured pens, pictures, paper and glue. You may laugh, but trust me, I've yet to see a team not get swept up enthusiastically in an activity where they get to create something together.

During this interactive exercise you all reflect on a time when you worked in a high-performing team. You think about what it felt like, how you behaved and what you achieved. Using those insights, the group collectively refines their thoughts on what they believe to be the key ingredients for a high-performing team, and what they want this team to aspire to be. These might be expressed, for example, as *celebrate success, clear vision, future focused, aligned* or *driven*.

These ideas are then displayed—pictorially and in words—on your vision board. This vision board can be displayed where the team works (I've even seen it turned into a screen saver picture), becoming a point of reference and a reminder of what the team has agreed to work together to achieve.

Purpose without supporting behaviours is meaningless.

Agreeing on how you work

As the leader you set the behavioural tone and standards, and a key part of doing that is ensuring your team has clear team norms. You can think of these as a team charter, group agreements or principles that specify how you as a team have agreed you will work together.

These norms need to be developed collaboratively, because they represent your shared commitment to how you will work with each other and bring out the best in each other. They need to be statements that each team member, hand on heart, can live up to, and that you all agree to hold each other to account for.

Each team's agreement will be different, because it's about what your team specifically needs.

Here's what a team agreement could look like:

- We treat each other with trust, honesty and respect
- We support group decisions and don't try to undermine them
- We maintain confidences and have each other's back
- We understand our shared objectives and act on them collaboratively
- We always believe our teammates' actions are from a place of positive intent
- We seek to better understand the business context and use humility to achieve a win–win for the organisation
- We enjoy the journey together

I've used this approach with teams I've managed and with teams I've coached, and I find it always helps to provide clarity, consistency and certainty about how the team works together. Without it, it's easy for team members to hold varying assumptions about you and one another, and assumptions aren't helpful for anyone.

With your strategies in place, it's now time to take deliberate, purposeful and courageous action, which means stepping up to be the leader you can be.

On the field

Gary's expectations about leadership were characterised by professional distance, command and control, and respect for hierarchy. In the early years of his career he thought that approach worked. However, as times changed, he found his leadership style became less and less effective.

He wanted to be a better leader, so he listened to feedback from his team and began to involve them more. Over time, by trying out new approaches he shifted his leadership perspective. He came to realise it was about bringing out the best in team members and leaving people (not just processes and systems) in a better place than before.

Ultimately, by putting people first he got better results. That's your job as leader: to leave people in a better place because they've been led by you. Consider for a moment what might happen if you embraced this idea?

11 ACT WITH INTEGRITY

One of my favourite TED talks is Margaret Heffernan's 'Forget the pecking order at work'. In it, she shares the tale of biologist William Muir, who studied chickens to see how to make them more productive—that is, to lay more eggs.

He had two groups (or broods in this case), with the second brood comprising the 'super-chickens'—those from each of his previous observation groups that had produced the most eggs. By the end of six generations, what he found surprised him. The first group of average chickens were coming along fine—plump and healthy, and egg production was good. In the second group, though, all but three were dead as the survivors had pecked the rest to death!

Margaret's point is that most organisations have been run according to the super-chicken model. (Perhaps literal fatalities have been avoided, though some of us might at times feel like we've been pecked to death.) She explains, 'We've thought that success is achieved by picking the superstars, the brightest men, or occasionally women, in the room, and giving them all the resources and all the power. And the result has been just the same as in William Muir's experiment: aggression, dysfunction and waste.'

As the leader you play a crucial role in creating either a team of dysfunctional super-chickens or a team where every person brings their best self to work every day.

It starts with you building your leadership habits, so you are your best self at work.

Build good habits

Today's technologically driven workplace, where email, SMS, Slack and other forms of instant messaging services are displacing verbal communication, even for critical issues, is exacerbating the feelings of social dislocation and isolation at work.

> Human-to-human interaction is more important than ever, so you need regular practices or habits that fuel connection in your team.

Habits become ingrained patterns of behaviour, such that you need to spend less and less time debating or thinking about doing it; instead, you just get up and do it. Once something is a habit, we need to rely less on motivation or conscious thought to act.

James Clear, author of *Atomic Habits*, points out that 'the costs of your good habits are in the present. The costs of your bad habits are in the future.' When I look back at my time in corporate, I remember how initially I had this horrible habit of sitting at my desk and continuing to type on my computer when one of my team members came to talk to me. I thought I was being efficient and effective in trying to get two things done at once, but what I was really saying to my team member was 'I am too busy to talk to you'. They left feeling unvalued. It was a habit, thankfully, I learned to break.

By contrast, one of my former team members had this lovely habit of standing up if someone approached her desk to talk to her. By doing so she demonstrated to the other person that they mattered and she wanted to give them her full attention. It was a very powerful habit, and one I learned from her.

To get you started, here are my suggested top 10 leadership habits (and yes, many of these should go without saying, but sadly they are often habits that are missing in leaders):

1. **Be available**. Make time for your team. There will be occasions when you may need to change a meeting with a direct report, but when you do this regularly your team member feels undervalued and it can add to their stress levels.
2. **Be friendly**. Greet people when you come in to work in the morning. A simple 'hello' can go a long way and takes only a few seconds.
3. **Be interested**. Take an interest in your team at a personal level. Find out what matters to them by asking about their interests, family and

other things of importance to them. Get to know, and acknowledge, their birthdays and other significant milestones.

4. **Get connected**. Wander the floor and check in on people to see how they are doing. Sometimes, rather than sending an email, make a request or give a response in person. There are times when this is also a faster way to action a piece of work. If you work remotely, regularly ring your team members for no other reason than to say 'hello' and check in on how they are.
5. **Pay attention**. Focus when a team member or colleague is speaking to you. Give them your undivided attention, and don't answer phone calls or respond to emails during the conversation. If they come to your desk, stand up to greet them.
6. **Be responsive**. Respond promptly to all emails and phone calls from your team. If time doesn't permit this, then have someone in your team who can respond on your behalf. When you ignore someone's request for help or advice you are setting the standard that it's okay to ignore the people you work with.
7. **Be appreciative**. Be courteous and appreciative of your team's efforts. It doesn't take much to say 'please' and 'thank you', yet in email communication it can often be forgotten. Pick up the phone and say 'thank you' and 'well done'. This small effort will demonstrate you have noticed what they do and acknowledged that their efforts matter.
8. **Be their coach**. Look for opportunities to support your team members. Recognise that people want choice and autonomy, so provide the encouragement for them to come up with solutions, rather than giving them all the answers. Be interested in their growth and development, and check in regularly to see how they are tracking. Ask them what more they need from you.
9. **Share success**. Be genuinely happy about your team members' achievements; always be ready to share the glory and acknowledge their efforts. Find ways to elevate your team members' successes.
10. **Own your liability**. If you've made a mistake, fess up. Role model by accepting responsibility and looking for learnings.

What are the top 10 daily leadership habits you need to put in place to be a better, more effective leader?

Avoid the stereotypes

As you start trying out and adopting new habits, you may encounter challenges and pushback because of stereotypes around what it means to 'be a leader'.

Leaders often say to me that they've been told they have to:

- be certain and never show or admit to any doubts
- act as though they have all the answers
- be in control of what's going on
- keep their emotions and feelings in check
- remain emotionally distant and not build friendships with team members.

The stereotype is of a strong leader, likely a charismatic extrovert. In today's working world, the stereotypical macho, all-powerful, all-knowing leader just doesn't cut it.

Throughout history, the best leaders have forged their own path. Take the remarkable Ruth Bader Ginsburg, for example, whose life was recently dramatised in the movie *On the Basis of Sex*.

The daughter of first-generation Jewish immigrants, Ruth was born in March 1933 in an unassuming house in Brooklyn, New York. She lost her sister to meningitis when she was 14 months old and her mother to cancer just before she graduated from high school. She studied at Harvard, became the first female member of the *Harvard Law Review* and graduated from Columbia Law School, becoming a staunch advocate for the fair treatment of women. She was appointed to the US Court of Appeals in 1980 and eventually the US Supreme Court in 1993.

Throughout her career, Ruth encountered hurdles and discrimination because she wouldn't conform to what women were expected to do. At Harvard she was one of just nine women in a class of 500 men. The Dean at the time famously asked, 'How do you justify taking a spot from a qualified man?' During this time, she supported her husband's study while he fought with cancer. She juggled her work and his work while looking after a young child.

In 1959, despite graduating first in her class at Columbia, she struggled to find a job. When she entered academia, she was told she'd be paid less than her male counterparts for the sole reason that her husband had a well-paid job. She was one of only 20 female law professors in the US at the time, but that didn't deter her.

She challenged rules that didn't make sense and went on to forge her own successful path as a leader. She succeeded despite all the prejudices aligned against her.

Being a great leader isn't easy. As part of your new leadership practices you need to check the rulebook you are following regularly to make sure it is fit for purpose. And when it's not, be ready to change it.

Be willing to throw away unhelpful and outdated leadership orthodoxies.

Check your expectations

Think about the last time you hired someone for a role. What's one of the first things you did? It's likely you rang someone you know to get feedback on the person you were thinking of hiring.

It's a sound, logical step, right? When we are hiring people or moving to a new leadership role, we often seek other people's opinions on a person's performance. This sense check can help you better understand a person's capability, their fit with the team and whether they may perform well in certain roles. Yet remember that as individuals we all thrive under different types of leaders and leadership.

Reflecting on when I was a corporate leader, for example, there were times when a colleague's well-intentioned feedback on a potential team member turned out to be wrong. People who were labelled and pigeon-holed as a certain type of employee turned out to be star performers in the team.

If you haven't taken the time to get to know deeply each member of your team, their strengths and their weaknesses, it can be easy to quickly, and incorrectly, label the team's 'stars' and 'laggards'. This can negatively impact how you lead and interact with the team.

Research conducted many years ago by psychologist Robert Rosenthal revealed this disconnect. He looked at the impact a teacher's expectations can have on a student's performance. In the experiment, teachers were given the names of students who were expected to do well through the year. These names, however, were picked at random, which meant those selected were no brighter than other students in the class.

His research found that the teachers treated these students differently. They were more supportive and friendly towards them. They were also more willing to spend time with them and provide them with feedback. Not surprisingly, the performance of these students improved.

> You need to suspend judgement of people, and constantly check your expectations to ensure you are treating your team members fairly and without bias.

TIME OUT

- How can you ensure you are being fair with the expectations you place on each team member?
- Do you have preconceived ideas about particular team members? If so, how are these clouding your judgement or how you treat them?
- What actions do you need to take so you treat each team member with the same level of care and attention?

Bring out their best

In his book *Lost Connections*, Johann Hari highlights the impact that boring, monotonous and meaningless work has on people. It impacts their mental health, wellbeing and outlook on life, particularly when they don't feel valued and appreciated.

The New York Times columnist and author Charles Duhigg cites research that shows substantial declines in worker job satisfaction, from about 61 per cent in the mid-1980s to around 50 per cent today. He attributes the drop in satisfaction to 'oppressive hours, political infighting, increased competition sparked by globalization, an "always-on culture" bred by the internet and … an underlying sense that their work isn't worth the gruelling effort they're putting into it'.

Despite all the changes in the world of work—how we work and what we do—our desire for meaningful and purposeful work hasn't changed. We want to add value and to be valued. You can't create this environment unless you know what motivates and inspires your team members, what they enjoy and what they don't.

All roles have elements of drudgery to them, so this isn't about not acknowledging that fact or ignoring the work that needs to be done. It's about finding new ways to make the work interesting, and where possible getting your team to help shape the nature of their job description and the work they do.

This means regularly sitting down with your team and asking them about their favourite projects, the moments when they feel most inspired and engaged, and the areas in which they would like to hone and develop their skills.

It's about working with the strengths of your team members and identifying their weaknesses or areas for improvement.

Research conducted over the past 30 years shows that this kind of strengths-based approach to leadership generates greater work satisfaction, engagement and productivity. This is evidenced in Tom Rath and Barry Conchie's book *Strengths Based Leadership*.

Tom Rath's StrengthsFinder tool is an excellent resource for conducting a strengths-based assessment across the team. It is based on four domains of leadership strength: *executing*, *influencing*, *relationship building* and *strategic thinking*. No style is characterised as better than another. In fact, healthy and balanced teams will present a mix of strengths.

This is a great team activity to do together. Once everyone has completed the assessment, you can have a conversation about how each person uses those strengths at work. It's as simple as asking each team member to consider 'I am at my best when …' and then to share with the team the environment that brings out their best.

This activity is a lovely way to increase rapport, trust and connectedness. Once you know the strengths of each team member, and they know each other's strengths, it is easier for people to collaborate. This contributes to a collegiate and healthy team dynamic.

Alternatively, check out the VIA Survey of Character Strengths, a free self-assessment that helps individuals understand their strengths from 24 core characteristics. The greatest strength is listed first, and the least is listed last. The insights generated from this exercise can be useful in a variety of settings.

Remember, to be your best, you need to take action to bring out the best in your team.

Let them be them

It's natural to want to work with people you like and find easy to collaborate with, so when you are building a team or work group you often seek out such people, but as we've explored already, diversity is good for you. This means you need to avoid the trap of trying to turn your team members into carbon copies of you.

Francesca Gino, a behavioural scientist at Harvard Business School, surveyed more than 2000 employees across different industries and found that many employees feel a pressure to conform. More than half the respondents said they did not question the status quo. Her research found that organisations encourage employees to leave part of their real selves at the door, which leads to decreased engagement, productivity and innovation.

When people feel compelled to conform to certain ways of working you lose the best of who they really are, and you are at risk of losing valuable team members.

> People have different working styles and behaviours. Sure, some of them may annoy or frustrate you, but you need to give them a chance to do it their way.

TIME OUT

- How can you better empower your team members?
- What would you need to change for your team members to have more autonomy?
- How are you encouraging each team member to be themselves?

Leadership is facilitation

In your leadership role you may not realise it, but you facilitate (or at least you should) all the time. In his book *Facilitator's Guide to Participatory Decision-Making*, Sam Kaner explains how the facilitator's job is to support everyone to do their best thinking by encouraging participation, promoting mutual understanding and cultivating shared responsibility.

As a leader, your role is to facilitate conversations and to make sure everyone feels safe to contribute ideas.

Think about it. Have you ever been invited to a meeting or forum where the pretext was consultation or seeking feedback, yet when you attend there is far more talking *at* you than listening *to* you?

The intent may have been genuine and well-intentioned, yet you walk away scratching your head and wondering why you bothered, because your concerns, ideas or insights weren't heard. Unfortunately, this is all too common in so-called stakeholder forums whose purpose is claimed to centre on 'feedback', 'listening' and 'consultation'.

This is veneer consultation — also known as 'window dressing' — with no real desire to listen or engage. Such an approach may allow you to check off another item on your to-do list, but it doesn't achieve buy-in or build team connection.

Your people need to feel and know they are being heard. They want their voice to matter, to feel genuine involvement and connection. For this to occur, important meetings and workshops should be deliberately structured to ensure the most effective participation and gathering of ideas.

You can't facilitate if you aren't ready to listen. That requires you to be present — focused on the person talking, with no distractions — and to be genuinely interested and curious about what they have to say, asking questions and seeking clarification before sharing your own ideas or providing a solution.

The next time you are planning a workshop or discussion, consider these seven tips:

1. **A fluid agenda.** While it is outlined in advance, the agenda is open to adjustment, based on what the participants on the day need to get out of the conversation.

2. **Open timing.** The timing of the session is structured around the participants' needs. At the start of the session you seek to uncover the participants' hopes and expectations from the session and you adapt the flow of the session accordingly.

3. **No predetermined outcome or hidden agenda.** You don't have a predestined outcome that you must achieve from the conversation, because you are open to all ideas on the table.

4. **A range of processes and activities.** Workshop activities are designed to ensure there is a range of ways for people to share ideas and provide

feedback. This should take into account different communication styles and comfort levels in speaking up in a large group format.

5. **Feast mindset**. You approach the session with an open heart and mind so you can see and sense what is being said and unsaid in the room, and ideas, insights and concerns are surfaced in a way that everyone who attends feels they have contributed and their voice has been heard.
6. **A safe space**. All participants should feel safe and comfortable to share, debate and contribute to the day's discussions. This means you do not shut down dissenting opinions; rather, you are curious about all ideas presented.
7. **A facilitated approach**. You create the environment that supports discussion and debate by being a facilitator, not the chair of the meeting. This means you listen empathetically, with compassion and without judgement.

Sure, some of this can feel a little scary — particularly having an unstructured and fluid agenda — but by taking this approach you are far more likely to get the outcome you are looking for.

Find time for you

When all is said and done, if you are working in a job you don't like, working in a toxic culture and for an overdemanding boss, then you will struggle to be a good leader. Similarly, if you don't take care of yourself then you'll struggle to have the bandwidth to cope when things go haywire, and unproductive leadership behaviours will surface.

When you are stressed and unhappy you are not at your best, and it's likely that those around you will suffer the fallout.

You need to be in peak physical and mental condition. So if you are stressed or feeling like you're struggling with a difficult boss or demands, revisit Part I to check in on how you are taking care of yourself and what you need to do to help you cope.

Just as you want your employees to be their best, you need to bring your whole and best self to work every day.

On the field

Gillian had been working very successfully at senior levels. She was respected across the board ... then a new boss arrived. Rather than focusing on leading the team, much to Gillian's frustration the new boss got bogged down in the technical aspects of the function. He wanted to be involved in everything — every decision, meeting, email. It was micro-management on steroids!

Gillian felt hamstrung, disempowered — and frankly embarrassed, as she felt her boss's behaviour indicated a lack of trust, and that he didn't think she could do her job.

Eventually, when the situation showed no signs of improving, she resigned. Happily, she quickly found another job (with better pay), but the organisation and boss lost a key talent and years of knowledge — all because he wasn't willing to loosen the reins and trust an experienced and proven team member.

It's a reminder that as the leader your actions have consequences — and some might not pay off for you in the long run.

12 REFLECT ON GROWTH

In the 1937 Disney classic *Snow White and the Seven Dwarfs*, the Evil Queen is obsessed with being the best. Every day she stands in front of the magic mirror and asks, 'Mirror, mirror on the wall, who's the fairest of them all?'

It all goes swimmingly so long as she hears, 'Queen, *you* are the fairest in the land'. It goes downhill big time, though, when she gets feedback she doesn't want to hear. One day the mirror responds, 'Snow White is the fairest of them all' ... and the Queen goes nuts. Snow White becomes the object of her hatred, and she plots to have the young girl killed.

It's a classic tale of good versus evil, and a lesson that it's not what's on the outside that's important, but what lies within us. Outwardly, the Queen is beautiful, but inside she is vain, insecure and filled with self-loathing and hatred for possible rivals (definitely a famine mindset!).

She's also completely unprepared for unwelcome feedback. It's a classic case of 'shooting the messenger' (or in this case destroying the mirror then plotting to take out her rival). Workplaces are often competitive and political, and it can be easy to get caught in the comparison trap and to think that to get ahead you need to win, to beat all rivals, to be 'the best'. Yet success in life, and at work, isn't about beating everyone else; it's about being *your* best, which means any competition should be with yourself.

Check in regularly to see if you are being your best, and if you like what you see in the mirror.

Mirror, mirror ...

Throughout Part III, you've been challenged to close the gap between your leadership promise (what you want to do and be) and your leadership practice (what you're actually doing and being). This next step is where the old adage 'What gets measured gets done' comes into play.

The legacy you create for your team members will be positive or negative, depending on the effort and dedication you've put into becoming an effective leader, and sustaining that effort.

Let's start by identifying the progress indicators you can use to continue to reflect on how things are going. As in the economy, there will be leading and lagging indicators.

> Indicators will alert you to warning signs of decline, and potential and real progress.

Your leading indicators point to the progress underway because they track your leadership habits and practices, including, for example:

- spending more time with your team
- having more regular one-on-ones
- finding a better balance between focusing on task and focusing on people
- having more regular feedback sessions.

Lagging indicators, on the other hand, confirm that a pattern of change is in progress, or has been made (or not made). These are data sources. Lagging indicators may include:

- higher engagement levels
- a decrease in turnover
- increased productivity
- lower error rates
- less stress and sick leave or unplanned absenteeism in the team.

Lagging indicators will come from 360-degree feedback assessments, engagement and employee satisfaction surveys, employee staff indicators (such as turnover, absenteeism and sick leave) and key performance indicators (such as quality, performance, productivity, revenue and sales). Typically, they take more time to access and require a dollar investment, so may not be readily available.

TIME OUT

- What data sources are available that you can use to assess your progress?
- How frequently can you access that data — daily, weekly, monthly, quarterly or annually?
- What does the data tell you about how you are doing?
- What does it tell you about where you could improve?

Setting up indicators is only helpful if you build a regular routine of checking the data, then spend time working out what it is telling you.

It can be easy to manipulate data to tell a story that makes you feel comfortable, so for this exercise to be helpful, be open to what you see in the data and get curious about the possibilities and potential for further change and progress.

Progress takes time

Making progress isn't about one big thing you do. It's about the things you do every single day. Some will be tiny, others big; some quickly noticeable, some not.

Leadership development is an ongoing journey of discovery. The learning never stops. Equally, be prepared for progress to take time. While you may notice some shifts around the edges quite quickly, most change takes at least six to 12 months of sustained effort to translate into tangible benefits and outcomes.

> Don't be put off or disappointed if progress isn't as fast as you'd like it to be.

One of my clients was a great manager, but it was only when she went through a formal feedback process that she discovered her leadership was failing. Her team and peers found her distant and hard to connect with, overly driven and ambitious, and too willing to say 'yes' to the needs of people more senior than her.

Over a 12-month period she dramatically turned her profile around. She spent more time with her team, which helped them get to know her, and her them. She built deeper relationships with her peers and stakeholders, reaching out proactively to help them and connect. She shifted her approach and behaviour, and as a result how she was viewed as a leader changed.

Success comes more easily when you see the benefits it brings, and you can feel the positive energy and impact you are having. In fact, it feels so good you'll just want more of it. And why wouldn't you? When you know you are creating an environment where every person in your team can be their best—well, that's liberating and empowering.

But be careful of becoming complacent and falling back into old patterns of behaviour, particularly when you are tired and stressed.

You are creating new leadership muscle and it will take a while for this to become habitual.

Five traps to trip you up

As I did throughout my corporate career, and now in my executive coaching work, I often see leaders who are trapped. They know something's not working but struggle to pinpoint what it is. They are locked in a pattern of thinking and behaving and are fearful of change.

It often takes a crisis—getting fired, facing redundancy, a major illness or another life-changing event—that forces them to stop, reflect and recognise that it can't go on like this anymore. Obviously, you don't want this to happen to you, so you need to be aware of five traps that can trip you up.

1. **The ambition trap**. For leaders who are used to success and always doing well, success can be addictive. They don't know how to step back from striving for it, and when the pressure at work rises their solution is just to work harder and keep going. If this is you, you worry that if you take your foot off the accelerator you'll no longer succeed.
2. **The expectation trap**. For leaders who are constantly living up to the expectations that are placed on them by those around them, admitting they are struggling and overworked seems impossible. They are so focused on doing what they are expected to do, they never get around to doing what they can do. When the pressure gets too much, they hide the impact and never share how they are feeling. If this is you, you worry that if you admit you are tired and struggling people will think less of you.

3. **The busyness trap**. It was Socrates who said, 'Beware the barrenness of a busy life.' Leaders who are caught up being busy and always 'on' struggle to say 'no', to slow down or to switch off. When the pressure gets too much, they are likely to explode as they are already close to burnout. If this is you, you will likely regularly sacrifice time with family and friends and even your health for work. Work comes first, and you see being busy as part of who you are. Be aware that this isn't a sustainable approach and eventually your body will force you to stop.
4. **The translation trap**. Many leaders have worked hard to get to their position, yet once they get there they find they aren't as happy as they thought they'd be. They feel like they are lost in translation: they wanted the role, but now they've got it the role doesn't fulfil or inspire them. If this is you, you'll feel like you have lost your way and your purpose. At the same time, you worry that if you change course you'll make the wrong decision, or that you don't know how to change because you think that what you currently do is *all* you can do.
5. **The self-care trap**. Many leaders get by on adrenaline alone, not taking enough time to care for their mind, body and spirit. They forget that putting their self-care needs first is a critical act of leadership. If this is you, then you are likely to feel run down, tired and overworked, and you say to yourself 'I'll get on to this tomorrow', but tomorrow never comes. One day you'll wake up and find that exhaustion, adrenal fatigue or some other health issue stops you in your tracks.

These traps are not discrete and isolated. In fact, they frequently overlap. When you fall into one or more of them the impacts may include social isolation and dislocation, poor health outcomes, negative impacts on team members, deteriorating social and family relationships, and over time a negative impact on your career outcomes and therefore your career prospects.

Are you in danger of falling into one of these traps?
If so, what needs to change?

Culture check

As part of this reflection process, and being aware of the traps, it's important you look at how your organisation's culture is impacting you.

TIME OUT

- Are you proud of the organisation's culture?
- Is the organisation's culture having a positive impact on your leadership?
- Does the organisation's culture enable you to bring your whole and best self to work every day?
- Are there times when you find yourself stepping away from who you want to be as a leader in order to try to fit the organisation's culture?
- Are there aspects of yourself you need to hide from your team members, peers, boss or colleagues for fear of retribution, recriminations or exclusion? Can you be authentically you?

Every day you need to check in and ask yourself: Am I being authentic and living true to my leadership vision?

Every time you step away from who you want to be, ignore the problem and fail to treat the impact, you are deepening the risk of permanent long-term infection. As an inoculation strategy, you have two options:

1. Find a treatment strategy to minimise the impact
2. Find an exit strategy to remove yourself from the impact

Your treatment strategy involves determining how you can influence the organisation's culture in a way that supports you.

This might include, for example:

- talking with your boss about any impacts their behaviour is having on how you work. (Part I will help here.)
- finding time each day to centre yourself, and at the end of each day asking yourself, 'Did I hold true to my vision and values today?'
- deliberately removing yourself from conversations or decisions that don't align with who you want to be.

- having a coach or a trusted colleague who can highlight when you may be about to sidestep (or have sidestepped) your leadership vision and values.

If there are no available treatment strategies (or you've tried them and found they don't work for you), and you want to ensure you retain your integrity and mental wellbeing, then you need to consider whether it's time to activate an exit plan from the organisation. This may not mean you move to another organisation; it may mean finding a new boss or role (my book *Career Leap* could help you with that).

> This is a critical test of your willingness to live up to your leadership potential.

Be truly coachable

Being willing and open to new ideas, new possibilities and new ways of doing things also means being willing to test and learn from your mistakes.

'A good leader,' Margaret Heffernan counsels, 'knows she's not perfect and doesn't mind her team knowing it. People don't want perfection, they want consistency. Besides, knowing that you're fallible makes people trust you more ... because they know you're human, just like them.'

> It's not about being perfect; rather, it's about continuous improvement.

Andre Agassi was one of the world's best tennis players. Throughout his career, he had some amazing highs with spectacularly good tennis days, while on other days he would come crashing down.

In his autobiography, *Open*, he recounts a conversation with his coach Brad Gilbert. This was at a time when his game was faltering. His coach told him that his problem was 'perfectionism'.

He said, 'You always try to be perfect, and you always fall short and it fucks with your head. Your confidence is shot and perfectionism is the reason. You try to hit a winner on every ball, when just being steady, consistent, meat and potatoes, would be enough to win ninety percent of the time.'

Agassi learned the value of listening and being coachable. He pushed through the challenges, and accepted that to achieve his goals, he had to uncover what was holding him back, try new things and then forge through. And look where that took him: he eventually won eight Grand Slams!

You can't do this on your own, however. You need to surround yourself with trusted advisers and a great support crew.

Build your support crew

Who do you trust? Who do you turn to for guidance? Who can you safely share your struggles and challenges with?

It's imperative to have a support crew, who act as your trusted advisory board. These are people you can call on for advice, support, counsel, and objective and constructive feedback. It might include a former boss, a current work colleague, a mentor (either internal or external to your organisation) or your partner. They need to be willing to challenge you, to hold up a mirror to show you whether your assessment of your progress isn't too rosy or misaligned.

These supporters can play an essential part in helping you sift through the feedback and assess how you can use it to carry you forward. They can help reality check your interpretation, pick you up and encourage you to keep going if you find progress slow and hard.

They can call you to account when you aren't living up to your stated values and are sidestepping courageous conversations. And they can help if you reach a point where you feel stuck or trapped and things at work just don't seem to be working.

It's critical to surround yourself with the right support crew who will back you and challenge you.

Don't stop

Being a leader is a privilege, and with that comes a whole lot of responsibility. You get the chance to shape, nurture and encourage the leaders of tomorrow. How awesome is that?

So don't stop. This has been a big chapter of reflection and revision. You'll have noticed progress and identified where you want to do more. Perhaps you've needed to challenge yourself to step outside and look beyond where you are currently.

You may also have discovered that you have some work to do in the relationship with your boss, in which case you'll want to go back and revisit Part I.

Remember the wise words of Benjamin Franklin, one of the world's great polymaths: 'When you're finished changing, you're finished.'

On the field

Jason was a senior manager for a large industrial company with national responsibilities. The role was complex, with competing demands, shifting stakeholders and a restless team.

After feedback from his boss about his leadership style, and its negative impact on the team and their performance, he accepted that he needed to change.

To develop his vision of the leader he wanted to be, he spent time thinking about the best leaders he had worked with and the ones he admired from afar. He also got input from his team members on the type of team they wanted to be a part of.

Using those insights, he constructed a plan to shift his leadership and the team dynamic over a six- to 12-month period. He tried out some things that didn't quite land as expected, so he continued to seek regular feedback from his team and boss. He was open to new ideas. He practised, got comfortable with being uncomfortable and implemented daily leadership habits.

Over time, his leadership style shifted to being more inclusive, authentic and transparent, and the team's performance lifted as a result.

What would a similar approach mean for you and your team?

WHERE TO NEXT?

In his 2018 Year in Review, entrepreneur and philanthropist Bill Gates shared how his perspective on life had changed as he aged. He explained how the questions he asked himself at 63 were very different from the ones he asked when he was in his twenties.

In his twenties, his end-of-year assessment was all about Microsoft and whether the dream of personal computing was coming true. 'Today,' he said, 'I still assess the quality of my work. But I also ask myself … Did I devote enough time to my family? Did I learn enough new things? Did I develop new friendships and deepen old ones?'

I love this reflection because it's a reminder that what matters to us changes as we progress and evolve — not just as employees and leaders, but as people. What won't change, however, is the desire to work in an environment where your contribution has meaning and purpose, where you feel valued and you can be your best.

The workplace can be challenging and complex. So why would we want to compound the pressures by not creating the right support mechanisms and practices to allow everyone to thrive and excel? When everyone plays their part in the relationship dynamic, it creates the opportunity for the leadership pressure chamber to have a fully functioning release valve.

When it's working well, the workplace works, and everyone steps up feeling match ready.

That's why progress for you isn't about taking time out to skim through this book, and thinking, 'Check. I'm done'. The process of assessing, strategising, acting and reflecting is continual, and always changing, because your perspective will keep changing as you progress through your career — into different jobs, workplaces and leadership positions.

Your mission — should you choose to accept it — is to hold true to your values always, to learn constantly and to put your best self forward so you inspire those around you to be their best too!

A MESSAGE FROM MICHELLE

Regardless of the level you occupy in the organisational hierarchy, you have the opportunity to step up every day and lead. And often the person you most need to lead is YOU.

Bad Boss was designed to be a book of hope, not hatred. A book to help, not hinder your progress. A book to inspire, not intimidate.

My wish for you is that this book has challenged, encouraged and galvanised you to embrace a new way of feeling, thinking and acting so you are your best, and that this inspires others to do likewise.

If you are committed to reaching your best and living to your full potential each day, then it doesn't stop here.

The best books are referred back to often, a constant source of reflection. They are dog-eared, annotated and highlighted, shared with friends, family and colleagues.

Sometimes, though, books aren't enough. If you find you want more advice or guidance than you have found here, reach out to me at:

michellegibbings.com

When I am not writing, I'm speaking at global conferences, facilitating leadership and team sessions, and mentoring — always with the deep desire to instil in people like you the courage, capability and conviction to bring their best selves to work every day. And in doing that create happy, healthy and thriving workplaces.

Here's to you — being match fit and going for the goal every time!

Michelle

SOURCES

Introduction

Bernstein, Ethan, Bunch, John, Canner, Niko, and Lee, Michael (2016), 'Beyond the holacracy hype, *Harvard Business Review*, July–August.

Brown, Lauren (2019), 'One in three workers "afraid to raise issues with their manager", survey reveals', *People Management*, 9 May.

Casserly, Meghan (2012), 'Majority of Americans would rather fire their boss than get a raise', *Forbes*, 17 October.

Clifton, Jim (2017), 'The world's broken workplace', Gallup, 13 June.

Godin Seth (2019), 'Leadership', Seth's Blog, 16 August.

Harter, Jim (2019), 'Why some leaders have their employees' trust, and some don't', Gallup, 13 June.

IBM Institute for Business Value (2015), 'Myths, exaggerations and uncomfortable truths'.

Lebowitz, Shana (2016), 'The "Big 5" personality traits could predict who will and won't become a leader', *Business Insider*, 8 December.

McKinsey & Company (2010), 'Strategic decisions: When can you trust your gut?', March.

McKinsey & Company (2019), 'Happiness and work: An interview with Lord Richard Layard'.

Powell, Robyn (2016), 'Half of all Australians experience workplace bullying, survey finds', ABC News, 9 October.

PricewaterhouseCoopers (2014), 'Creating a mentally healthy workplace: return on investment analysis'.

Study Finds (2018), 'Do you? 1 in 5 employees admit they HATE their boss', 21 April.

Chapter 1

Battelle, Nora (2018), 'How to handle the stress of a bad boss', *Thrive Global*, 17 October.

Brown, Brené (2018), *Dare to Lead*, Vermilion, London.

Douglas, Emily (2019), 'Is your boss a corporate psychopath?', *Human Resources Director*, 17 July.

Chapter 2

Watkins, Michael (2003), *The First 90 Days*, Harvard Business Review Press, Boston, pp. 108–9.

Chapter 3

Breines, Juliana (2015), 'Four great gratitude strategies', *Greater Good Magazine*, 30 June.

Donigian, Aram, Hughes, Jonathan, and Weiss, Jeff (2010), Extreme negotiations', *Harvard Business Review*, November.

Inesi, Ena, Pfeffer, Jeffrey, Sherman, Eliot, and Sivanathan, Nliot (2018), 'Power play', London Business School, 13 August.

Klein, Gary (2007), 'Performing a project premortem', *Harvard Business Review*, September.

TRIPOD (no date), 'Stress hardiness', stresscourse.tripod.com.

Chapter 4

Brown, David (2015), 'Here's what "fail fast" really means', *Venture Beat*, 15 March.

Di Stefano, Giada, Gino, Francesca, Pisano, Gary, and Staats, Bradley (2014), 'Learning by thinking: How reflection improves performance', Harvard Business School, 11 April.

Kellogg Insight (2015), 'Fake it until you make it? Not so fast', Kellogg School of Management at North western University, 3 August.

Chapter 5

Artz, Benjamin, Goodall, Amanda, and Oswald, Andrew (no date), 'If your boss could do your job, you're more likely to be happy at work', getpocket.com.

Benson, Alan, Li, Danielle, and Shue, Kelly (2018), 'Promotions and the Peter Principle', NBER Working Paper No. 24343, National Bureau of Economic Research, May.

Grant, Adam (2018), 'Wondering', www.adamgrant.net, August.

Heifetz, Ronald, and Laurie, Donald (2001), 'The work of leadership', *Harvard Business Review*, December.

van de Loo, Erik, and Cools, Kees (2019), 'For the truth about how bosses behave, ask their assistants', *INSEAD Knowledge*, 30 January.

Patterson, Jim (2015), 'Study: Bad middle managers are just a reflection of their bosses', Vanderbilt University, 26 January.

Pearce, Craig, and Manz, Charles (2014), 'The leadership disease . . . and its potential cures', *Business Horizons*, 57(2), pp. 215–24.

Shapiro, Jonathan (2018), 'WCM Investment's $36b bet on culture', *Australian Financial Review*, 1 June.

Chapter 6

Bissinger, Buzz (1998), 'Shattered Glass', *Vanity Fair*, September.

EurekAlert! (2019), 'Good grief: Victimized employees don't get a break', 8 March.

Kellogg Insight (2010), 'Better decisions through diversity', Kellogg School of Management at North western University, 1 October.

Noer, Michael (2014), 'Read the original Forbes takedown of Stephen Glass', *Forbes*, 12 November.

Sull, Donald, and Spinosa, Charles (2007), 'Promise-based management: The essence of execution', *Harvard Business Review*, April.

Chapter 7

Edmondson, Amy (2018), 'How fearless organizations succeed', *Strategy + Business*, 14 November.

Chapter 8

Horn, Jonathan (2019), 'Richmond demolish GWS Giants in AFL grand final', *The Guardian*, 28 September.

Schmook, Nathan (2017), 'Revealed: Three words powering Richmond', AFL Media, 30 September.

Chapter 9

Coetzer, Michiel, Bussin, Mark, and Geldenhuys, Madelyn (2017), 'The functions of a servant leader', *Administrative Sciences*, 7(1), 24 February.

Covert, Bryce (2019), 'The richest man in China is wrong. 12-hour days are no "blessing" ', *The New York Times*, 21 April.

Definition of servant leadership (no date), toservefirst.com.

Edmondson, Amy (2019), 'Creating psychological safety in the workplace', *Harvard Business Review*, 22 January.

Eurich, Tasha (2018), 'What self-awareness really is (and how to cultivate it)', *Harvard Business Review*, 4 January.

Heifetz, Ronald, and Linsky, Marty (2002), 'A survival guide for leaders', *Harvard Business Review*, June.

Kellogg Insight (2015), 'Why bad bosses sabotage their teams', Kellogg School of Management at North western University, 5 January.

Keltner, Dacher (2016), 'Don't let power corrupt you', *Harvard Business Review*, October.

Laseter, Tim (2016), 'The line between confidence and hubris', *Strategy + Business*, 21 November.

Porath, Christine (2014), 'Half of employees don't feel respected by their bosses', *Harvard Business Review*, 19 November.

Sachdeva, Sonya, Iliev, Rumen, and Medin, Douglas (2009), 'Sinning saints and saintly sinners: The paradox of moral self-regulation', *Psychological Science*, 20(4), pp. 523–8.

Chapter 10

Ibarra, Herminia (2003), 'Working identity — nine unconventional strategies for reinventing your career', *Harvard Business School*, 2 October.

Kellogg Insight (2010), 'Better decisions through diversity', Kellogg, 1 October.

Kellogg Insight (2015), 'Fake it until you make it? Not so fast', Kellogg School of Management at Northwestern University, 3 August.

Sendjaya, Sen (2017), 'Why Australian businesses need to become servant leaders', Monash University, 27 June.

Tenpas, Kathryn Dunn (2019), 'Tracking turnover in the Trump administration', Brookings Institution, October.

Chapter 11

Duhigg, Charles (2019), 'Wealthy, successful and miserable', *The New York Times Magazine*, 21 February.

Gino, Francesca (2016), 'Let your workers rebel, *Harvard Business Review*, October–November, p. 2.

Heffernan, Margaret (2015), 'Forget the pecking order at work', TED Talks.

Wilkinson, Alissa (2018), 'On the Basis of Sex', *Vox*, 25 December.

Where to next?

Gates, Bill (2018), 'What I learned at work this year', Gates Notes, 29 December.

INDEX

CPSIA information can be obtained
at www.ICGtesting.com
Printed in the USA
JSHW040015150521
14779JS00005B/205

9 780730 383970